THE GREEN PLATFORM

DECLAN COYLE

THE GREEN PLATFORM
SIMPLY LIFE-CHANGING

Ballpoint Press

*To our special son, Alexander, who was born and lives on
The Green Platform and brings so much unconditional love,
fun and spontaneous joy with his infectious laugh.*

*To Annette, his mother,
Genevieve, his sister
and Fionn, his brother.*

Published in 2013 by Ballpoint Press
4 Wyndham Park, Bray, Co Wicklow, Republic of Ireland.
Telephone: 00353 86 821 7631
Email: ballpointpress1@gmail.com
Web: www.ballpointpress.ie

ISBN 978-0-9550298-8-2

While every effort has been made to ensure the accuracy of
all information contained in this book, neither the author
nor the publisher accept liability for any errors or omissions made.

Book design and production by Elly Design

Cover photograph courtesy of Alltech

Printed and bound by GraphyCems

Contents

ABOUT THE AUTHOR

DECLAN COYLE is a director of Andec and one of Ireland's most internationally experienced leadership training and development consultants. He is also much sought after as a conference keynote speaker.

His success as a top-class inspirational speaker for business leaders has in recent years been harnessed in the sports arena where he has given regular goal-setting and mental strength motivational sessions to a number of GAA teams including the successful Kerry and Cork (football), Tipperary (hurling), and Dublin (hurling) teams. He worked closely with Kilmacud Crokes when they won the 2008 All-Ireland Club Championship.

Declan is himself a former Ulster Championship medal winner who played senior football with Cavan.

He also worked with the Kentucky Wildcats when they won the National Basketball Title in the U.S.

A former Columban missionary for 27 years, Declan is married with three children and lives in Bray, Co Wicklow.

He writes a weekly motivational column for *Fit Magazine* that is published with the *Irish Independent*.

Declan is a member of the Irish Institute of Training and Development. He is also a Master Practitioner in NLP and a certified Enneagram teacher.

Introduction

"Everyone on the face of the Earth has a treasure that lies waiting for them."
Paulo Coelho, The Alchemist

SOME years ago in the US I got on a bus outside the Hilton Downtown Hotel in the heart of Lexington, Kentucky with a close friend to go out to the Alltech FEI World Equestrian Games at the Horse Park.

My friend was there as a guest but he doubled up his visit with an attempt to get me to write a book on the power of 'The Green Platform'. He believed that if people understood the concept of getting off the negative disempowering Red Platform with its "poor me" victim-stories and changed their mindset over to the positive "can do" empowering solution-focused Green Platform, it could instantly transform people's lives for the better.

There are only two massive influences in our lives, positive things or negative things. I have positive thoughts and feelings or negative thoughts and feelings. In our daily lives, we do these two things over and over. We think and we feel. We either think and feel about all the negative things we don't want to create and attract into our lives on the Red Platform or we think and we feel about all the positive things we want to create and attract into our lives on the Green Platform.

I cannot control many of the situations that happen to me in life, but I can control how I respond to what happens to me. Like traffic lights, when you see Red (negative), stop. Green (positive), go. The quality of my life for better or for worse depends on which platform I choose – the positive, uplifting, constructive Green Platform or the negative, miserable, destructive Red Platform.

Probably the greatest challenge of our times is to empower people to step off the Red Platform and on to the Green Platform. Why?

Over the past 40 years across every developed country in the world the diagnosis of clinical depression (a sure sign of Red Platform living) has grown nearly tenfold. This has happened despite the fact that almost every factor we associate with happiness and well-being on the Green Platform – plentiful food, money, education, safety, access to art, literature, music, gyms, swimming pools and health care – is abundant in these societies. More and more people are reporting symptoms of life on the Red Platform – feelings of restlessness, fatigue, stress and a sort of malaise that leaves them feeling bored, unsure or frustrated. The Red Platform is full of what Melville of Moby Dick fame called "the horrors of the half-lived life."

Social Psychologist David Myres gives us this shocking review of our addiction to the joyless malaise of "the half-lived life" on the Red Platform: "Whether we base our conclusion on self-reported happiness, or rates of depression ... our becoming better off over the last 30 years has not been accompanied by one iota of increased happiness and life satisfaction. It is shocking, because it contradicts our society's materialistic assumptions, but how can we ignore the hard truth: once beyond poverty, further economic growth does not appreciably improve human morale. Making money, the aim of so many graduates and other dreamers of the 1980s, does not breed bliss."

We desperately need new tools and a new way of living. We need to find ways, strategies and tactics to eschew this poisonous way of living that does not "breed bliss" on the Red Platform, and to switch to the Green Platform.

What's on the Green Platform? What's underneath the Green Platform?

On the Green Platform you are inspired and you live with joy, inspiring others as you bring joy into their lives. You are engaged, energised and enthusiastic. It's on the Green Platform that you will find the treasure that lies waiting for you as you discover your passion, find your true purpose in life and follow your dreams so that you can make a real contribution to humanity.

You are living your truth, and actualising your potential as you follow the true north of your own inner compass. You are real. You are authentic. You are valid. On the Green Platform you are genuine – not wandering around with a fake perma-smile pretending that all is well when it's really not. You are genuinely, straight from the heart – optimistic, positive and constructive.

Underneath the Green Platform is the field of all possibilities where you discover creative solutions to life's challenges. It's where you unleash your true potential to be the best that you can be, to fuel every moment with the best that's in you now.

That morning over coffee in the city centre hotel, my friend told me it wasn't so much for me or himself that he felt we should undertake this project.

"There are so many ordinary people out there who would benefit from knowing about this simple concept," he declared. "You owe it to those people to put pen to paper and show them how it works." Then he really drove his point home. "You're like a man with the cure for cancer entering a room full of cancer patients. You have the cure. But you won't give it to them. Why? Because you have your little bag of excuses."

Of course I had. I told him I was very busy in the US and the UK with work as well as at home in Ireland and finding time as a family man would be a major challenge for me.

Sometimes though the logic of a situation is put in perspective by something unforeseen. An omen. A sign. A hidden message. That's what happened within half an hour of that chat over breakfast. To go out to the Horse Park, we had to get on shuttle buses that Alltech, the company sponsoring the FEI World Equestrian Games were running in order to cut down on traffic snarl-ups. We were the first two on the bus on what was a sunny autumn Kentucky Tuesday morning.

The next passenger on was a blonde lady in her mid-twenties who greeted us with a warm smile. "Sorry for delaying you," she said in English (but I immediately detected a Dutch accent).

Within a few seconds I remembered she had been on a course I had given back in Ireland a few years beforehand. In fact I also remembered her name. It was Annette. The same name as my wife – Annette. This young lady's full name is Annette van Lochem and at the time she was an Alltech employee.

As I was frantically trying to recall the exact details of that previous meeting, I could see by her that she was going through the same process in her head. What followed next, in the context of my earlier conversation was amazing.

"Declan, isn't it? Yes. Do you know the Green Platform totally changed and transformed my life ... in so many ways!" she said.

Talk about a dramatic statement. When I looked at my friend, I saw a knowing look in his face as if to say: "See."

Slam-dunk, game, set and match all rolled into one. His argument had been delivered with whatever sporting terminology you would like to use. For me, probably a knockout is the best description.

But that wasn't the end of this remarkable morning's jousting.

A few minutes later, another lady, who chose to sit further back on the shuttle bus, got on before our driver jumped in behind the wheel and we departed. On the way out to the horse park we talked about the Green Platform moments and the situations where it had changed Annette's life. It shortened the journey and put me in the mood that maybe there was merit in what they were saying about writing such a book.

When we got off the bus, the woman who had decided to sit at the back, approached us with hesitant steps. She apologised, saying she has overheard all of our conversation on the way out.

"I was amazed to hear this lady say that the Green Platform had changed her life. What is the Green Platform? Is there a book on the Green Platform? Where could I get it?"

My friend put his arm around the woman, asked her for her name and said he would send her a complimentary copy when it was published.

Pointing a finger at me, he said with a mock-seriousness to his tone. "You sir, get writing. How many omens, signs or inner nudges do you need to get the wheels in motion?"

Over the following days and weeks, I found Annette's statement that the concept of The Green Platform totally changing her life as an inspirational message that I could not let go.

So, this then is the story of the Green Platform and its power to change and transform lives. I hope it helps you as thousands of people have told me the concept has helped them to change their lives for the better since I first used it in leadership, team-building, personal development courses and keynote presentations over the past 18 years.

I live it every day and find it underpins virtually every decision I make, every feeling I allow to develop into an action.

*   *   *

To get on the Green Platform, you need a key. It's called awareness. You would be surprised in our busy lives how seldom we have that key in our hand.

We mostly allow ourselves to be led passively onto the reactive Red Platform where we see life as something out to trip us up at every turn.

However, it need not be that way.

In the following pages you will see how to access the Green Platform and stay there. You will also become aware of how the negative Red Platform sneaks up on all of us – and how to avoid that happening or get off it when we find ourselves loitering there.

CHAPTER ONE

The Green And Red Platforms

EVERY morning and indeed many times throughout each day, you and I, often totally unaware, make a decision to use either the Green or Red Platforms.

You might well ask – what is the Green Platform? Or what is the Red Platform? They are terms that can on one hand show how imprisoned we are to our own limiting thoughts; on the other hand they can show you how to change and utterly transform your life for the better.

How do they work? First let's look at the Red Platform, the negative, self-sabotaging platform.

Every day over 50,000 thoughts go through your head. Most of these – 40,000 or 80 per cent – are negative. It means that for every one time we have a positive Green Platform thought, there are four occasions when we land on the Red Platform in negative mode.

So why do we see Red and why do we get on the Red Platform?

Every time we decide to blame or complain or start telling a victim story such as: "It always happens to me" – we are on the Red Platform. That means most people spend 80 per cent of their time on the Red Platform, thinking negative thoughts day after day. Normally 95 per cent of the thoughts we have today are the same as the thoughts we had yesterday.

THE ABCS OF THE RED PLATFORM
The ABCs of the Red Platform are Anger, Blame and Complain. When we are in this state, we use words like "you" or "they" or "he" or "she" to blame outside forces for our life circumstances. Underneath this platform, there is a tank of fuel called fear. When we are born we land on the Green Platform and all we have in our Green Platform tank is love. As we grow up we gradually learn all

about fear and fill our Red Platform tank with it. If we look for a personality or a figure emerging out of this tank of fear and living on the Red Platform, we find the Ego.

THE EGO

We've all heard of him (or her). We say people have big Egos as if they are proud of themselves. But in reality the Ego is a sham. It is a false self who works night and day – if you let him or her – to undermine your state of happiness. The Ego's main weapons are fear, anxiety and doubt.

The Ego works his or her socks off to keep us away from joy and happiness in the present moment – the now. Like Dracula's inability to live in the light, the Ego cannot live in the present. It stalks your mind by reminding you of how stupid, clumsy, inappropriate you were in the past and fuels your thoughts with fear anxiety and worries about what is down the line waiting for you in the future.

So as a shadow cannot live in sunshine and darkness cannot live in a room when I turn on the light, the Ego cannot live in the present moment. Once we become aware of that and bring awareness to the present moment, we have a great weapon to undermine the power of the Ego, reclaim our lives and get back on the Green Platform.

That key word – awareness – dismantles the power of the Ego and gets us on the Green Platform. The real you lives on this powerful positive platform while the Ego lives on the Red Platform feeding on fear, anxiety and doubt.

The key is to become awake, aware and alert.

We become aware by activating our "Inner Observer", our "Alert Watcher", our "Witnessing Consciousness". In a word you must become your own "Noticer." If you manage that, it means you will be able to notice the shenanigans and manipulations of the Ego as it strives to keep you from your joy and happiness in this present moment.

The Ego allows us to think that we can be happy – but only somewhere way down the line. It never, ever will help or enable you to be happy in the here and now.

The Ego is a very important player in all our lives. And if we don't wake up and realise the damage it is doing to us on an hourly, daily and weekly basis, he (we'll call him "he" for handiness sake) will continue to be the orchestrator of our worries, fears, sadness and real suffering.

Like all forces of darkness, the Ego is manipulative, clever and persuasive, particularly if you don't stand up to him by the simple act of bringing awareness to recognise his underhand activities.

The Ego invites you to step onto the Red Platform by reminding you of the mess you made in work yesterday or the way your boyfriend or girlfriend is fed up with your behaviour. Once the Ego gets you on the Red Platform, he has you snared.

Expertly, he will then go to work by filling your past with shame, anger or guilt. He is equally happy to project you into the future where he will highlight your areas of worry, fear and anxiety about financial problems or personal relationships or whatever area he perceives to be a weakness in your attitude.

Imagine you are driving to work or on the train or on the bus or maybe you are just in the kitchen and this invisible hand of unhappiness is prompting you to bring resistance and non-acceptance to your life as it is now.

Before you know it, the Ego has you making up imaginary fights with your boss, your boyfriend, girlfriend, husband, wife or partner. Once you're on that Red Platform, he is winning and knows his job will be easy for the rest of the day. The Ego is one of the few who is happy when he sees Red. He is at his happiest when you are at your unhappiest.

He will prompt you with whispers of: "My boss is always picking on me," or: "I do everything around here," and without your knowing it, you are winding yourself up at a rate of knots. Tense, unhappy, wearing a scowl on your face. He is a grievance looking for a cause and too often we unwittingly help him find that cause.

The Ego is your deadliest foe in life – the enemy within. If you can understand that and then become aware of the Ego's negative influence on your life, this is the first serious breakthrough.

There is an old African proverb that says: "If there is no enemy on the inside, the enemy on the outside doesn't matter."

I found it groundbreaking the first time, many years ago, when I was made aware of what prompts so many of my thoughts and negative attitude in the course of any given day.

In the intervening period, I have had the need every day to stop and realise that the Ego is still there, trying to coax and cajole me onto his home base – The Red Platform.

And, of course, sometimes he still wins. But at this stage I'm catching him more quickly now. The one thing we know for sure is that awareness is power. Often when I find myself slipping into victim mode about something, the simple thought clicks into my mind: "This is the Ego trying to fool me."

I can then jump from Red Platform to Green Platform literally by thinking that one thought. Bringing the light of awareness to the darkness of the Ego's behaviour.

A little miracle occurs in your life every time you realise that.

Once we decide to put up our hand and say: "Enough. I will decide how I will live my life today," we get a power into our life that is simply amazing.

Like all miracles, it is just a simple change in attitude that brings a massive change in how we can enjoy our lives. Each one of us must reclaim our own lives by being aware of what makes us unhappy (the Ego's agenda) and learn how to be happy and in control of our own destiny.

Here is another little sentence that packs a real punch if we are to truly reclaim our lives.

The best way to understand life is to accept it.

To be one with life. Once you see the value of acceptance then you apply what I call the PAN formula ... acceptance plus Positive

Action Now. Acceptance without positive action could easily degenerate into indifference or apathy. So in a time of adversity, step one is acceptance.

It is as it is.

You cannot argue with reality or you will lose – 100 per cent of the time. We love to use the words "should" or "shouldn't" in a way that challenges reality.

"I should be getting that job," or "This shouldn't be happening to me."

But it is as it is.

Step two is a powerful question that implies action: "Of a list of 100 items, what is the one thing I can do now to make this situation better? What is the one thing I can do to improve it?"

Then do it.

If it is a fine day, smile and enjoy the sunshine. If it is a rainy morning when you look out, it should not mean that you believe everything that happens you will be gloomy for the rest of the day.

We are like that. We say: "What a dreadful day. And I feel terrible as well."

What's dreadful is the toxic little story we are telling ourselves in our heads about the day. Now, tell me, if you write that headline for your day ahead, do you think you have any chance of having a fun-loving and happy time?

Highly unlikely.

That's the Ego at work. You open the curtains or pull the blinds and instantly it makes up a story about the day.

"That's a dreadful day."

This is a toxic influence that we must eradicate from our systems. If we don't, we can't find the bliss of living on the Green Platform on a day-in, day-out basis.

The three shadows of the Ego are then, next, and more.

"When I lose weight, then I'll be happy."

But not now. Never now. Losing weight is not the key to happiness – happiness is the key to losing weight.

When I get this or that, then I'll be happy.

Then ... next week.

Next June.

Next year.

But never now.

Or "more." When I get more time off, more pay, more holidays... then I'll be happy.

But not now.

The Ego is quite literally that fearful thought that happiness is not and never will be in the present moment. If today you could just bring the power of awareness to your life, the Ego will disappear like a shadow in sunshine.

The only place we will ever live is in the present moment. We live in a continual present and if you are enlightened enough to realise that and say: "Right now I have no problem," then you are going to have much more joy in your life than someone who looks around corners.

You are becoming an empowered person. You are breaking free from that reactive prison of the Red Platform and landing on the proactive Green Platform with 10 of the most powerful words in the English language, no word more than two letters: "If it is to be, it is up to me."

You have discovered responsibility. The ability to choose your response. You'll discover on the Green Platform that the happiest people do not have the best of everything; they just make the best of everything. On the Green Platform you realise that life is not about getting what you want but rather wanting what you get. This is the major difference between success and happiness. Success is getting what you want. Happiness is wanting what you get.

Then taking positive action that will transform your life situation. The ultimate gift of the Green Platform is to be able to live life as if we didn't have an Ego.

THE ABCS OF THE GREEN PLATFORM

That brings us to the ABCs of the Green Platform: Awareness. Belief. And Commitment.

We have now come to understand that awareness is activating your "Inner Observer" where you become the "Noticer" in your life. You observe what's going on in your mind without judgement. With judgement your Ego is back in control. Your "Noticer" should never be the "Judgemental Noticer", but the "Compassionate Noticer". Compassion that does not include you is not compassion.

Belief and the power to break limiting beliefs. Whether you believe you can or you can't, either way you are usually right as Henry Ford reminded us years ago.

Commitment is to do what I say I'll do long after the mood that I said it in is past. It's about a steely discipline. It's about keeping your word to yourself. As Thomas Huxley said many years ago: "Do what you should do, when you should do it, whether you feel like it or not."

Underneath the Green Platform is the field of all possibilities. That's where we find a new and a great and a wonderful world. It is a joyful place of creativity and inspiration where you contribute and make a difference in the lives of people.

The 'Real You' on the Green Platform says: "How can I serve others and add value to their lives?" The 'False You,' the Ego on the Red Platform says: "What's in it for me?"

On the Green Platform you contribute to relationships and the other person leaves you happier and more energised. You see each relationship as an assignment. You are an energy transformer.

People on the Red Platform contaminate relationships. They suck your vital energy with their complaining, whining and blaming. They are energy vampires.

When you make a choice you change the future. Decisions shape destiny. The choices you make, make you. It all comes down to a choice. One of your greatest hidden gifts is your power to choose which platform you want to land on and live on, no matter what happens in your life. How come we spend so much time on the Red Platform? Part of the reason is that we spend a huge amount of our time on automatic, reacting to events, but not really consciously choosing our response.

CHAPTER 2

The Colour Of Your Day?

IF we are truthful, we find ourselves more often on the Red Platform than the Green Platform. Why is that? Why do we spend so much time on the Red Platform?

Well, we've grown up with it. All our lives we've watched our parents complain, give out, become paranoid about issues. "Tidy your room", "Do your homework", "Sweep the floor", "Put the dishes away", or "Brush your teeth".

So it's second nature for us to take up the negative cudgels of our parents. It's an acquired family habit. Have you ever noticed that families tend to have similar traits? Apples don't fall too far from the tree. I've heard myself turn into my father. As I've grown older and had my own family, I've started to speak like him. Now I give out about the same things he used to, like the unnecessary use of electricity.

"Lights on everywhere. Will someone turn off the lights when they leave a room," I hear myself say. He died in 1987, or as he said himself shortly beforehand, he "crossed the great divide", but he's still alive and well ... in my head.

I've caught myself saying things I said I'd never say to my children. Those old scripts that we are surely recycling since the 14th century are alive and well in me.

"I'll tell you once and I'll not tell you again."

That never worked with me – yet I recycle it.

"How many times must I tell you?"

And I love this one. It never made any sense to me, and yet now I'm using it.

"Why?"

"Because I said so."

What kind of an answer is that? Then there was the old crying one. "Stop that crying or I'll give you something to cry about."

It dawned on me as I've heard what I'm saying that maybe I should turn the light on in my own head. We parents tend to come across as negative influences in our children's lives. We give out about the mess our kids leave in their rooms, the way they get up at the last minute for school or sometimes we show displeasure at the way they dress or behave.

Let's just pause here for a second. These are the people who are the nearest and dearest to us. Yet we are ingrained with the need to be negatively attacking them at every turn.

If the Dalai Lama comes visiting and spills some milk on the table what will I say?

"Don't worry, your holiness, sure it's only a drop of milk." And I mop it up and hand him a tissue to pat his robes down.

If one of the children does the same thing, what kind of a response will they get? There is a good chance we give them a dressing-down and bring in a whole number of misdemeanours that show them up in a bad light.

Does it make sense?

The only difference is that we love our children much more than we love the Dalai Lama. Why do we give a Green Platform response to the Dalai Lama and a Red Platform response to our children? The ones we really love. When you notice these centuries old scripts coming up again and again, ask yourself: "Do these handed down scripts serve me or my family well?"

Mindful of how easy it is to slip into habits handed down to us through generations, can you from now on make a few small decisions that will have a major positive influence on your life?

The first is to dare or at least consciously try to be happy and joyful each day. How do you do that?

By simply deciding that you are going to step onto the Green Platform and stay there come hell or high water.

A decision. A choice. Consciously made. Cutting off any other possibility.

When the Moors pulled the boats into the harbour and landed in Spain, their leader asked them were they committed to fighting the Spanish?

"Of course," they replied.

"That's fine," the leader said, "then burn the boats."

That was a decision with commitment.

A Green Platform decision. Making a choice – creating the future. Your decisions shaping your destiny.

A Red Platform decision is holding on to the usual way you think in a manner that sabotages your attempts at positivity. And if you always do what you've always done, you'll always get what you've always got. If you want different results, you do different things. The Chinese say that insanity is doing the same thing over and over again and still to be expecting different results. Einstein had the same idea.

Once you decide to actually like yourself and your day, you break the Ego's spell.

So much of our anger and frustration with others comes from wanting and expecting them to be something other than what they are. We want to rewrite their stories and make them into what we think they should be. It's the Red Platform Ego with its judging conditional love rearing its ugly head again.

There's a version of the Serenity Prayer that captures this:

"Grant me the serenity to accept the things I cannot change. (It is as it is.)

The courage to change the things I can. (Bringing awareness to the Ego. Acceptance plus Positive Action Now.)

And the wisdom to know the difference."

If we turn that into a people version we might end up with something like this:

"Grant me the serenity to accept the people I cannot change. (They are as they are.)

The courage and awareness to change the one I can. (Guess who?)

And the wisdom to know it's me."

That last line is important because ultimately the only one I can really change is myself. The mistake we make is we try to change those around us in the hope that it will improve ourselves. But that is putting the cart before the horse.

I remember one time interviewing a very holy old white-bearded Rabbi in Birmingham. "When I was ordained a young Rabbi," he said, "I wanted to change the world. Then I decided some years later just to focus on Europe. Some years later I decided to focus on London. As I grew older I decided to focus on changing my congregation. Then as years went by I decided to focus on changing my family. Then my wife. Finally I got it. The only person I can really change is me." That's why blaming other people is so impotent, because no matter how much I blame you, it will never change me."

"And the wisdom to know it's me."

Gandhi put it well: "Be the change you want to see in the world."

On the Green Platform you actually become like an orange. If you squeeze an orange what comes out of it? Orange juice. Why? Because that's all that's in it. Orange juice. Not lemon juice. Not apple juice. Not pear juice. Just orange juice.

If inside you there is only the peace, joy and happiness of the Green Platform, then it doesn't matter who puts pressure on you, or tries to stress you out, or "squeezes" you in any way or pushes your buttons, all they will get is peace, joy, happiness and unconditional love. Why? Because that's all that's in you.

But if you are living on the Red Platform full of anger, bitterness, and resentment and somebody "squeezes" you, that's all they will get out of you, because on the Red Platform, again, that's all that's in you.

On the Green Platform you set the agenda that is capable of "changing me, and being the change I want to see in the world."

I can go on a diet and eat an organic lettuce leaf and a cracker, but if on the inside in my heart I'm planted on the Red Platform, vicious and vile and spitting out negativity ... what's the use of my organic diet?

To keep us from being fully present here and now, happy here and now is the Ego's agenda and that's how he makes sure that joy eludes us now. Maybe later, but not now. Never, ever now.

Once I decide to live on the Green Platform today and be happy here now, the Ego has no choice but to go off into the corner and curl up.

There is an immediate spin-off for you when you make the bold and brave decision to be happy today. Simultaneously, you will help make those around you much happier as well; whether it is a husband, wife, mother, father and especially children, over whom you have a profound influence. The greatest gift you can give to your family or friends is a positive emotional state.

In the Irish language we say: "Tús maith leath na h-oibre" (a good start is half the work). It is actually from the moment you wake up that you must start to change the rest of your life.

A friend of mine said recently he finds the first three minutes after waking up the most crucial period of his whole day if he wants to step on the Green Platform.

Those initial 180 seconds after we rouse ourselves are the key to deciding which road we travel for the day and which platform we enter the day from. Red or Green?

There is a real choice to be made.

Mostly our minds seem to automatically default to the Red Platform. Years ago at home when you'd come across someone who was cranky, contrary and miserable, people would say: "He got out on the wrong side of the bed this morning."

We know now that such a person landed on the Red Platform.

As my friend explained to me: "For those first few minutes after I wake up, my mind is invaded by a posse of negative thoughts. They are like a battalion of soldiers surrounding my head. Their mission appears to be to defeat you before you gather your thoughts. But if you decide to jump into the shower, force yourself to laugh for five or 10 seconds and declare (whether you believe it there and then or not) that you are going to have a great day, the negative soldiers disappear and with them your Automatic Negative Thoughts (ANTS). That's my friend's view and his way of handling the first big test of his day.

By forcing himself to laugh he sends a message through his body that he is happy. He then sees himself having a joyful day. That mental image also sends positive messages around his nervous system.

He is activating a mechanism called the Self-Fulfilling Prophecy. It's a powerful mechanism. I first heard about it from my mother many years ago. We hear all kinds of tribal folk wisdom when we are growing up in our families. I grew up in Dungimmon in Co Cavan, a beautiful valley between the ancient wisdom hill of Loughcrew and that famous romantic lake, Lough Sheelin, forever linked with the love story of Orwin and Sabina, whose commitment to each other was stronger than their family quarrels.

Some of this tribal wisdom and 'sayings' we paid heed to. Others we didn't. My mother used to say: "There is so much good in the worst of us and so much bad in the best of us that it ill-behoves any of us to talk about the rest of us."

Quite a mouthful but laden with great wisdom. She was saying that none of us is any better than the next person. Another thing she used to mention a lot was the power of the self-fulfilling prophecy. "If you believe you'll fail, you'll fail. If you believe you'll succeed, you'll succeed." A great summary of life on the Red Platform and life on the Green Platform.

In one of the most detailed studies on the effects of self-belief on performance, the Canadian psychologist Albert Bandura discovered that a person's genuine beliefs about their capabilities could be a more accurate predictor of their future levels of performance than any actual results they produced in the past.

It reinforces the power of the self-fulfilling statement: "The you you see is the you you'll be."

How you think about yourself in relation to the challenges you are now facing will have a profound impact on your ability to succeed. The story you are telling yourself inside your head, positive or negative, the little mental movies you are making will have an incredible impact on your ability to deliver on your working, recreational and health goals.

This mechanism is what my mother years ago called, "the self-fulfilling prophecy." It's one of these phrases I've heard about for years, but never fully unpacked to discover the real depth of meaning it contains.

For instance, if someone believes they are ugly and unattractive and that no one could ever be possibly interested in them, how would you expect them to behave?

If they see someone that they are attracted to, are they likely to approach them in a confident manner with a spring in their stride? No.

Having this negative belief about themselves means they won't take actions to disprove it. In fact, they bring about the very condition they wish didn't apply and in a perverse sense prove their negative belief to be true.

They'll conclude that's there just no point in even trying which in effect fulfils their prophecy. What they don't know is that their mind or Ego wants to be right all the time. The mind loves a "What did I tell you?" response. The Ego will sabotage any level of success in order to be "right," and convince you that you are no good and that you'll never amount to much.

Sometimes that toxic question: "Now who's right?" creeps into families and workplaces. Again, that's the Red Platform Ego always wanting to prove itself to be right.

US social psychologist Leon Festinger had a good way of explaining it. He says that the state of trying to hold two inconsistent beliefs, ideas or opinions is so uncomfortable for the mind that we subconsciously try to reduce the inner conflict by changing one or both of our ideas so that they fit together better.

In other words, your mind wants to be consistent with whatever you previously said to be true. He called it "cognitive dissonance."

Your Ego mind is the original 'now, who's right?' stalwart. The 'what did I tell you?' person.

And of course the Ego-mind is at its most powerful when it's in negative mode, the prophet of doom predicting disaster. The best way to create the future is to predict the future.

"See, I told you you'd never amount to anything."

"You're a failure."

"You'll never get fit."

Similarly you cannot sit around resenting confident, successful people and be surprised that your mind doesn't want to join them. The mental transition from resentment to admiration is massive.

The best example of the power of the self-fulfilling prophecy is a story I heard one time from the US neuropsychologist and psycho-immunologist Dr Mario Martinez. He sometimes works with the church to reverse stigmata, where the blood flows from people's hands like Padre Pio – in imitation of the suffering of Jesus.

"When I discovered that the human mind could actually rupture skin, and create bleeding," he told me, "then I wondered what else it could do if we harnessed it?"

To demonstrate what he means, he recalled a great story from American football. Before the game, the groundsman came in to the two teams and apologised to them. He explained that he was training in a young assistant who, in a fit of enthusiasm in his first week, had sprayed the field with weed-killer before the game.

Normally, the weed-killer was only sprayed on the field after the game. The routine was to water the pitch first, and only after the game, when the players were safely on their way home did they apply the weed-killer. He told them that the side effects of the weed-killer would be quite mild, nothing much really, but maybe some of them might get a bit nauseous or maybe vomit, but nothing more serious than that.

After 20 minutes, the game was called off. Players were vomiting all over the field and feeling nauseous and returned to the dressing rooms. Then the groundsman came in. He apologised profoundly again to the players for misrepresenting what the new young groundsman had done.

As it turned out, he did exactly as he had been told. He only watered the field before the game. He just took the cans of weed-killer out of the shed and put them around at the gable of the dressing-rooms to be ready for spraying when the players had gone home. It was the groundsman's own fault for assuming he had applied the chemicals.

So there wasn't a drop of weed-killer on the field but the power of the Red Platform self-fulfilling prophecy is amazing. A real case of you'll see it when you believe it.

An editor will grab the attention of the reading public by writing a gripping headline. You could do the same for your day by writing your own positive Green Platform mental headline for the day and see how often it becomes a positive self-fulfilling prophecy.

Why don't you begin to develop your own way of meeting the day and deciding how you will literally make the best of that day? Don't just look at the clock startled when you wake up, complain that it couldn't be that time already and then slump back into the bed for 10 more minutes.

That will make you feel even more tired and behind the black ball when you do get up. You will be rushing, half-doing things when in reality, you should be gently stepping into the new day. Make it easy.

Get your own little positive routine going. Why not start by thanking God for all the blessings you have in your life. Then dare to be bold and write a headline for your day. Say I'm going to do things today that will give me a great lift. I will finish that report, come up with a plan for work or home or study something you have been avoiding that will make you happier.

Why not try to give yourself a break. Think about the way we probably wake up at present. Instead of feeling refreshed, we feel tired. We have something in work we are dreading or we have bills to pay and we are low on funds and we want to stay in bed, bury our heads and not get up 'til Monday.

The lift is at the Red Platform and it is easy to hear the voice inside telling you that you have no cause to press the button to go to the higher floor of the Green Platform.

"It's okay for the man writing this book but he hasn't got my problems," is, for instance, a great way for you to ignore this process and so not even make the effort to bring change into your life.

Isn't it funny how we feel everyone else's life is perfect and our own is a shambles?

It's all right for the rich people or the neighbours with two cars and two jobs. They can be happy but you can't.

Three minutes – a mere 180 seconds since you've woken up – and without realising it, you are programmed to have another negative day on this earth.

Growing up in Dungimmon, like everywhere else in Ireland, there were some days when we had good weather and some days we had bad weather.

I thought that I could do nothing about the outer weather around me.

I was right.

For years and years, I thought that I could do nothing about my inner weather either.

Some days I had good days and on others, many others, I had bad days that I thought I could do nothing about. Genuinely, I believed the problem lay with other people, other events or other situations. That was the easy unconscious way I gave my power away.

I was wrong.

Now, though, I have a different perspective on life.

I know that although I could do nothing about the outside

weather, I can do everything about my inside weather. It goes back to what I said at the start of this chapter... It's about realising we have the power to choose.

I can choose to have a good day on the Green Platform or I can choose to have a bad day on the Red Platform.

It's easier to stay in the position where all your worries about money or jobs or family take over. Then there is the postponed-happiness syndrome that we all seem to anchor in for large tracts of our life. For years I suffered from what I now call the "when I'm" virus.

"I'll be happy when I'm successful."

"I'll be happy when I have the mortgage paid off."

"I'll be happy when we get the holidays."

Here's a question that finally made me see things clearly when I put it to myself many years ago. "If you are not going to be happy right now, then exactly when are you going to let happiness into your life?"

When the children are reared? When you write a bestseller? When you win the lottery? Most of us have the habit of putting our happiness back until some vague time in the future.

You know what that means, don't you?

It means putting our lives on hold waiting for things next year or the year after. And deep down we know that it probably will never happen.

I have good news for you though.

Just because this is the way you think now, it doesn't have to be like that anymore. It is a habit and incredible as it sounds, we are comfortable with habits, even if it means not being happy with that habit. Every one of us is capable of living each day with happiness and joy. The single most radical, revolutionary act you can commit to in today's world is to dare to become a joyful person.

Could we dare to throw off the shackles of what we learned in the past and actually give our children the idea that some adults are actually enjoying themselves?

Could we dare to give up the habit of 'liking' our bad days?

Could we decide to live each day with joy? To give it a go? The goal of all goals is to enjoy the life you have been given and to be happy now. Not being happy here now is like giving a gift to someone and you know they don't like it. Your gift does not bring them joy or happiness. You give a similar gift to a different person and you see them wearing it and you can see clearly it has made them really happy. That, in turn, gives you a great feeling. The best response we can give for the gift of life is to be happy and joyful in our lives. Here. Now.

Try today to be grateful for everything? Happiness is a by-product of this. The pursuit of happiness in itself is a myth because it is nearly always somewhere down the line. The Ego loves the word "pursuit." It is not in the present time, the now, which is where we live.

What brings happiness and inner peace? Most people think the answer to that is to have loads of money. But once the basic needs are met, more money won't bring happiness.

Marriage won't bring happiness. Youth won't bring happiness. Great intellectual ability won't bring happiness. Nor will the weather bring happiness.

Happiness is all about your relationships and friendships and, of course, it is the by-product of pursuing some extraordinary purpose, some great project to contribute to the lives of other people.

Happiness is about the peace and joy and contribution you bring to those relationships and friendships. The most important and primary relationship is with yourself.

According to Irish Clinical psychologist, Dr Maureen Gaffney, in her book 'Flourishing', some 20 per cent of us are floundering, going around with a kind of low-grade depression. Sixty per cent of us are in ordinary mode, functioning. Sure we turn up for work but we just get through the day. Just 20 per cent of us are flourishing.

We are creative, joyful, spontaneous, innovative and everyone who meets us comes away happier, more positive and inspired. In other words, only one in five of us are really living on the Green Platform radiating joy, inspiring others, contributing to life and making a difference as we use our gifts and talents in the service of humanity.

The quality of your relationship with yourself and with others begins with your self-talk. Every morning we put in an imaginary CD into our heads. That CD contains our self-talk for the day. Which begs the important question – is your daily quota of self-talk positive or negative? Does your daily self-talk give you energy or sap your energy? Is it positive, uplifting and constructive ... or is it negative, belittling and destructive? As we saw earlier, on average 80 per cent of our self-talk is negative placing us firmly on the Red Platform 80 per cent of the time. Changing negative thoughts to positive thoughts is the first key to transforming your life from miserable on the Red Platform to inner joy, happiness and peace on the Green Platform.

We don't realise it but we need first and foremost to communicate with ourselves. If we feed positive thoughts on the Green Platform into our system, we will be energised and feel good. Conversely, if we are downbeat and negative, we are programming ourselves to a day's sentence on the Red Platform.

How life changing would it be for you if you said: "I'm opting to have a day of joy. And I'm opting for it now."

Not once-in-a-blue-moon joy. But right here, right now.

Remember "happiness"?

"If not here, where? And if not now, when?"

The next most important and secondary relationship is with others. How does this relationship affect our lives?

THE RED PLATFORM RECEPTIONIST

I remember a discussion I had with a receptionist in a workshop some time ago. I asked her what she did when she got an irate customer on the phone. She told me an instance of such a call from the previous week.

"Well, it was just after nine in the morning and I got this call. And this man screams and shouts and abuses me down the phone. Why me? It's the people in the warehouse he should be shouting at."

"How does that affect the rest of the day?" I asked.

"Well, that's my day shot. I was upset for the rest of the day."

She was firmly planted on the Red Platform. It was all his fault. Or was it? We all know how she feels. We've got such a phone call or dressing down in a meeting that has changed how we feel for the rest of the day. It could be a small comment or an NBR, a negative belittling remark.

Now ask: "What is happening here?"

We are giving a person, in this case an angry customer, enormous power over our lives and the quality of our lives each day. Until that call came in, she was in control of her day. She was, unknowingly, on the Green Platform. With that call she handed the driver's wheel over to some unknown voice and spent the rest of her day on the Red Platform. It leads to a general question: Where is the place of control and personal power in your life? Who has control of the switch? Is it inside you or outside you?

Your good day/bad day switch?

Your Green Platform/Red Platform switch?

Your Positive/Negative self-talk switch?

Is it outside you or inside you? Whose hand is on that switch all day, every day? You have your hand firmly on that switch. Up until that call she was driving the bus on her own life on the Green Platform, and then with one flick of the switch she jumped into the passenger seat and let someone else drive her through whatever slum he liked for the day. She had switched to the Red Platform. She had given her personal power away. Your personal power is in choosing your response to any situation by taking positive action on the Green Platform.

THE GREEN PLATFORM CUSTOMER CARE PERSON

I told that receptionist about a similar scenario I came across when I was giving a course in the US.

"What do you do when you get an irate angry customer shouting at you?" I asked.

A tall African-American stood up and smiled. "When I get an irate customer on the phone or face to face," he said, "that's when I shine!"

This man was choosing his response. He wasn't handing over the wheel to someone else to drive him where he didn't want to go.

I remember thinking at the time, in Ireland in a similar situation the response was, "That's my day shot!"

In the States, "That's when I shine!"

He had his hand on the switch of his own personal power. He was choosing the Green Platform. What are the specific steps or strategies we go though to get on the Green Platform? We'll look at this process next.

CHAPTER 3

White Space And The Power To Choose

MOST people fail to recognise that between something happening in our lives and our automatic response to it, there is a groundbreaking thing we can do.

We can enter into a White Space area and activate our power to choose. For many of us the idea of choice doesn't come into the equation. You get a slap from someone – you slap back; you get a smart remark from someone in work or at home and before you know it, you come back with one yourself.

"You're calling me stupid? You're not so hot yourself?"

"That's the pot calling the kettle black."

Or like Clint: "Come on punk, make my day!"

It is the stimulus and response syndrome ... stimulus and response. Like Pavlov's dog. Ring a bell every time you give him red juicy meat, and soon just ringing that bell has him salivating, dribbling and drooling.

Am I any different?

Am I a bunch of predictable reflexes like Pavlov's dog constantly being triggered by people and events into predictable outcomes on the Red Platform or can I creatively and proactively choose my response on the Green Platform. Have I got Green Platform response-ability? The ability to choose my response.

"He made me very angry." Pure Red Platform response.

No. He was jumping up and down like a Clydesdale horse gone mad, but I chose anger as my response. There are 50 different responses I can choose instead of anger.

Once you become aware of how futile it is to be a passive onlooker merely reacting like Pavlov's dog during the key moments of your own life, then you learn to proactively choose your response.

When I was working in slums in the Philippines, the single biggest question I used to ask them in our Action/Reflection/Action meetings was: "Are you going to continue to be passive objects of history or are you going to be creative subjects of your own history? Is life happening to you, or are you happening to life?"

After centuries of oppression I was challenging them come up with strategies and tactics to change their lives for the better.

Viktor Frankl, an Austrian psychiatrist and holocaust survivor, lived through the worst possible situations in life, including being a prisoner in the Nazi concentration camps. While he accepted that he was physically imprisoned, he told me years ago in Ottawa that he made the conscious choice from the beginning never to allow the Nazis to take control of his mind, his heart or his spirit.

He said that they could break his body ... torture him, but they couldn't take away "my power to choose." This power to choose he called the "the last and the greatest of the human freedoms." He said: "Between stimulus and response there is a space. In that space is our power to choose our response. In our response lies our growth and our freedom."

This was Frankl's amazing insight from the death camps: "Everything can be taken from a man or a woman but one thing: To choose one's attitude in any given set of circumstances, to choose one's own way."

He said that every moment of every hour of every day in the death camps he chose peace, joy and happiness inside. "They could break my body, they could torture me, but they couldn't touch my spirit." Though he never heard of the Green Platform he was, like so many thousands of great people that we know, living every day on the Green Platform. He was really years ahead of his time.

This was an immensely brave thing to do. In a different way, choosing your response can take bravery because the conditioned reaction comes so naturally to us that we don't even have to bother ourselves with thinking. Most of the time we're not even aware that we have a choice. We find it hard to see that White Space. We think people annoy us. We think people make us angry. We think people upset us. But we do have the power to choose. We do have Viktor Frankl's "last and the greatest of our human freedoms."

This was his great contribution to humanity. An amazing contribution that over the years we may have forgotten ... that a person is a choosing, deciding human being. Frankl firmly believed that "education must be education in the ability to choose."

Yet so much of our education takes away this fundamental tool to personal growth and development. So many people still live with a "tell me what to do and then I'll do it." Many teenagers are afflicted with this virus. You say: "Bring the dishes into the kitchen please." Then you go in and there they are on the worktop bench.

"Why didn't you put the dishes into the dishwasher?"

"Well, you didn't ask me to do that. You only told me to bring the dishes into the kitchen."

God forbid they might take initiative and go the whole hog and put them into the dishwasher.

"I don't know what you're complaining about. I did what you told me to do."

Somehow in our rearing and education systems we've knocked out that "Take initiative," "Proactivity," "Make it happen," "If it is to be it is up to me," aspect out of people. We make far too many decisions for people. As a parent one should never ever do for a child what a child can do for herself or himself.

In their 40s, two per cent of people are proactive and highly creative.

In their 30s two per cent of people are proactive and highly creative.

At the age of seven, 10 per cent of children are proactive and highly creative.

At the age of five, 90 per cent of children are proactive and highly creative.

Between the ages of five and seven we manage to blast 80 per cent of the creativity out of children.

In other words, between five and seven, 80 per cent of us who are highly creative develop an image or a picture or an attitude that we are not. We learn to paint and draw between the lines.

At age six, 95 per cent of children have a passion for possibility. But by the age of 12, they are firmly locked into limitation thinking. "I can't," is their predominant thought.

Test it yourself. Go into a kindergarten and ask the children, "Who here can sing?"

Watch as all the hands go up.

"Me!" "Me!" "Me!"

Then ask the same class of children at 12 years old.

"Who here can sing?"

"Well, not me. Britney, or Justin or Lady Gaga are singers. Definitely not me."

Frankl was right. Education must be education in the ability to choose. To decide. And that's at the core of the Green and Red Platform process. There are five steps:

STEP 1

Something happens that impacts on you. You feel it fully. You honour your human experience. If it's tragedy, you cry the tears or feel fully the fear, the loneliness or the joy. Then you detach from it and enter a White Space.

STEP 2

This is the place between stimulus and response where we have the power to choose our response.

STEP 3

We can choose the negative Red Platform where we complain and blame other people. This is the platform where we allow ourselves to negatively poison our thoughts, stories, images and beliefs.

The alternative is to opt for the positive Green Platform with its 10 most powerful words in the English language: 'If it is to be, it is up to me.'

This is the can-do platform with positive thoughts, stories, images and beliefs where we see ourselves achieving what we want to create and attract into our lives, and then manifest them in our lives.

This is the platform we land on as a result of this power to choose. The hope is that with awareness and conscious choosing, over time this becomes your automatic default platform of choice.

STEP 4

This step is the outcome or result. The outcome on the Red Platform is misery and self-created suffering. The outcome on the Green Platform is peace, joy and happiness here, now.

STEP 5

The outcome determines the quality of my life now ... joy, love and freedom on the Green Platform or fear, resentment and misery on the Red Platform.

But it all begins with Step One. Something happens. An event. You lose your keys or an aeroplane has engine trouble and your flight is delayed. The event always is as it is. The situation is always neutral. Then you choose your platform and the quality of your day will depend on which platform you choose. It's your call, your choice. Now I know that this is all right in theory, but how does it work in normal everyday situations? How does it work in practice? That's what we'll look at next.

CHAPTER 4

Unscrambled Eggs: The Life Lesson

ON the Green Platform we choose our response. On the Red Platform we react like Pavlov's dog. It's one thing to know what to do but it's quite another to do what we know. While I understood this intellectually for years since Viktor Frankl had talked to me about it, it was not until one incident with our daughter Genevieve that the power of "choosing my response" really hit home.

I describe it as the day she taught me how to unscramble eggs.

I'd say she was about five years old at the time and even then she was always trying to help. That is her nature, to be kind and generous and she is still has that same nature in her personality today.

But five year olds and handling eggs are not something that as a parent you want to put together in the one room.

She kept asking me: "Daddy, can I help you put the eggs in the fridge?"

I became more and more anxious as she inched ever closer to me with her hands out.

I tried to turn the container and myself out of her reach to put the eggs in the fridge.

"No, Genevieve, they are very fragile, I'll put them in myself," I said, raising my voice with enough authority in it to stop her in her tracks.

When I looked at her I could see the hurt on her little face. Holding back tears and with a little falter in her voice, she said she'd only wanted to help me. It was then I relented and gave her the two eggs I had in my hand and said, as all parents do: "Okay, but be careful you don't drop them."

Now anyone who knows anything about the subconscious and the way it controls 96 per cent of how we live and move knows that the subconscious doesn't process negatives. It won't process words like 'not,' 'don't,' 'instead of' or 'without.'

If I say to you, "Don't think of a red polar bear in the white snow of Alaska," ... then bang, the red polar bear is there in your mind in the pristine white snow. You get the picture. "Don't think of a white rabbit," and there's the white rabbit.

Your subconscious won't process the 'don't', as it won't process 'not' or 'without' or 'instead of'. Just like a heat-seeking missile it zones in on the picture. It just searches and looks for the picture and concentrates solely on that. The subconscious only processes pictures and the emotion tacked on to the pictures.

"Don't bang that door," means to a child, "bang that door and bang a lot more doors too."

The age-old law of attraction kicks in giving us more and more of what we focus on whether we like it or not and whether we know it or not. A mother will say to a child: "Be careful, don't drop that." and the child will drop it. Then the mother says: "I could see that coming. I knew that was going to happen. That's why I specifically told you not to drop it. You don't ever listen to me."

The problem is that the child listened.

To the subconscious of a child learning to ride a bicycle, "don't wobble." means "wobble ... don't."

So we see the Red Platform (RP) negatives that we are constantly challenged to change into Green Platform (GP) positives by focusing on what we want. Just keep asking that empowering Green Platform (GP) question: "What do I want?" Then focus on what it is you want.

So here I am in the kitchen with Genevieve.

What did I say to Genevieve? "Okay, be careful, don't drop the eggs." And then, bang on cue, she dropped them.

I can still see the look of sheer horror on her face after she let them fall. I was about to give her the same response that every generation of our family has given to their children who dropped precious eggs around my home place.

But something happened as I was about to launch out into the deep. You know the same old reactionary, negative, parental stuff that we come out with. Then we compound the situation by later trying to justify it, saying that it was "for her own good."

That little rider then absolves us from looking at ourselves and our inability to respond in a more appropriate manner. I could almost hear myself say: "Genevieve, I specifically told you not to touch the eggs. I told you they were very fragile. That's the problem, you don't listen. You never listen. Do you think I say these things just for the fun of it? Next time I want you to listen to me and do what I say."

However, I didn't rush into the usual download and say that. For some reason, I don't know why, at the very last moment instead of reacting I actually chose my response. I saw and entered the white space area between stimulus and response. In this tiny zone between seeing an action and then reacting to it, I realised for the first time in my life that I was in possession of an amazing power.

It was the awareness that I actually had a choice. In that "White Space" moment, I encountered the Viktor Frankl strategy.

This awareness gave me an immediate sense of genuine happiness and perspective so instead of feeling upset, I found myself looking at the egg-smashed mess on the floor. From my 6'2" frame I looked all the way down to the kitchen floor and said: "Genevieve, isn't that a very interesting design that the eggs have made on the floor. Do you think we should take a picture of it and show it to Mammy when she gets home?"

In that moment I consciously stepped off the Red Platform with full awareness and stepped on to the Green Platform. Even as a five year old, I could feel her sense of shock and then her relief at my response. In fact, she was so stunned that she squeezed her little arms around my knees, looked up at me and said with delight:

"Daddy, I love you."

What an instant payback.

Of all the things I remember in my life, that moment with Genevieve is right up there with the best. It was a life-changing incident for me and I don't think a day has gone by since that I don't remember 'the day of the scrambled eggs' and take something out of it.

The moral of this little story is all about choice. We do have the "power to choose" our responses in life. If only that one message gets across and nothing else, then this book will have been worthwhile.

I am not responsible for other people's reactions. I am totally responsible for my reactions. I am not responsible for what happens to me, but I am totally responsible for what I do about what happens to me.

Most of the time, most of us are just a bundle of conditioned reflexes reacting to people and events.

Did you ever see the behind-the-scenes person in a television studio who comes out and holds up a sign for the audience saying: 'Laugh,' or 'Applause,' and on cue the audience either laughs or claps.

Just like sheep. The farmers from around my home place in Dungimmon used to say that if one sheep went out through a gap from one field to another, the rest would follow. It's like they had no minds of their own.

Are we any different than these sheep? People don't annoy us. People don't make us angry. Most of the time we choose these responses and blame people and events. But no matter how much I blame you it will not change me. Whenever I point the finger of blame at you, there are three other fingers pointing back at me.

The power to choose our response and above all to choose the Green Platform is an enormous dormant power within us. We can become aware of that power we haven't allowed to develop in our lives and take control of our own destiny.

Are we driving the bus of our lives or are we passive passengers being swept along by other people's agendas and events?

So practise choosing your response. The best training ground you'll ever find is your family home. And remember every time you proactively choose a positive response on the Green Platform, the rewards are enormous. Like the huge reward I felt in Genevieve's response.

Then what happens in your brain? A new neuro-cortical pathway opens up and next time you're in a similar situation it's easier go down that pathway. Your brain is like a jungle. The first pathway will be difficult. The second time you go down that pathway it will be easier. Then slowly but surely, as you keep going down that "choosing your response" pathway, it becomes a habit. It's automatic.

CHAPTER 5

Flying When Your Aeroplane Is Grounded

THE scrambled eggs experience comes in all shapes and sizes. Let me give you an example we have all experienced at some time or other. You are at an airport either going abroad or trying to get back home. Minutes before you are due to board, you are told your flight has been cancelled because of the weather or a strike or a problem with the plane.

Your automatic responses go into overdrive. "I have a very important meeting to go to..." Or: "I have to get home to a big family celebration tonight." Or. Or.

The bundles of conditioned reflexes we have become begin to pour forth. Before you know it, you are suffused with righteous indignation and you can think of nothing else.

Only recently I was in a queue at O'Hare Airport in Chicago. I was behind a man who, like the rest of us, was told that our flight was cancelled. He went berserk. Not only that but he shouted and verbally abused the lady behind the desk, who had given us the news, as if she personally was responsible.

He glanced at me seeking moral support. By that time I had felt the first pangs of disappointment at missing a connecting flight to a very important meeting. Luckily my 'White Space' gap had clicked in.

"It is as it is." It was as it was.

I froze the essence of the moment as it was – the plane is cancelled. Full stop. Now I could take the example of the man in front of me and argue with the reality of the situation – which would get me nowhere because every time I argue with reality, reality will win 100 per cent of the time. I knew the best thing to do was to accept the situation as it was and then take positive action.

It is as it is and now I can choose to land on the Green Platform.

Can I accept the present moment as it is? Can I allow it to be as it is? Am I saying a deep Green Platform "yes" to this present moment as it is, feeling it deeply, or am I saying a deep and angry Red Platform "no" to this moment. The "is-ness" of the moment is a given.

The second step is to accept the present moment as if I had chosen it. (Not doing this won't change the reality, but doing this, accepting the present moment as if I had chosen it will change me.)

The third step is tough; can I embrace it? We create most of our suffering by our non-acceptance of life as it is. We suffer when we jump on the Red Platform, resist and say our deep "no" to life as it is. When we refuse to be one with life as it is. We cannot undo or rewrite the past. As the Iranian poet Omar Khayyam put it about 1000 years ago:

"The moving finger writes; and having writ moves on: Nor all thy piety nor wit shall lure it back to cancel half a line, or all thy tears wash out a word of it."

The event is over. Done. Dusted. Kaput. I cannot undo it or rewrite it.

There was only one indisputable fact at the airport... I would not be flying that day with that airline on the flight that had just been cancelled.

I had a choice in that moment of White Space between the bad news that I'd just heard and choosing my response. I refused to become a victim of the situation and instead chose to accept things as they were, and then looked for the one positive thing I could do to improve my situation. I activated the Green Platform formula of Acceptance plus Positive Action Now (PAN). Acceptance without PAN can easily degenerate into a resigned passive indifference or apathy.

A key point in moments like this is to ask a simple question: "Is there another way of looking at the present situation? What other opportunity is there in this event? What is the one positive thing I can do now?"

In other words, I stepped off the Red Platform and onto the Green Platform.

Naturally enough I felt at first the human feeling of disappointment and frustration, and then stepped mentally on to the Green Platform.

This is the first step of the Green and Red Platform process we saw earlier. You have a human experience. You feel it fully. You honour your human experience.

Then you detach from the situation and enter your White Space where you choose your platform ... Red or Green.

When the man, in an agitated state, turned to me to support his rantings, I told him if I thought for one second that all the shouting and negative belittling remarks could bring back or mend that plane, I'd shout and bawl with him all day. But it would not.

He then snapped: "Well, what are you so happy about?"

"No," I said. "I am not happy about it. I feel disappointed and frustrated. But this is not the worst news I could have received today. I'm in an airport so I have the chance to catch another plane with another airline. If not I will be put up in a comfortable hotel and even get some kind of a meal until they arrange an alternative flight tomorrow."

He waved a hand of disdain at my attitude. He refused to accept that "it is as it is" and stormed off to talk to some higher authority about the injustice he felt he had suffered.

I went across to another airline and within a matter of minutes found that I could indeed make the meeting by getting a flight to a nearby city where I knew I could hire a car and drive to where I wanted to go. As I was making my way through the airport, I saw some medical people rushing past me to a waiting zone.

Coincidentally, it was the man who had been complaining loudly in front of me some time earlier that they were attending. Now he was having some kind of a heart attack or heart palpitations because he had worked himself into such a state. So the last I saw of my Red Platform friend was his wheezing body on a stretcher being carried away.

I hope that whatever ailment he had was minor and that he made a full recovery. And I hope too, that he learned a lesson from his head-butting with reality ... a contest that is guaranteed only one winner.

What Viktor Frankl said about situations such as this was: "When we are no longer able to change a situation – we are challenged to change ourselves." If we cannot change a situation we change the way we think about a situation.

I'm not trying to say that these situations are easy. Such news can bring on stress but you only add to that by allowing your reactive reflex actions to take over and drive you half-demented. It is not reality that causes us stress; it's our story or perception of reality that makes us so unhappy.

When you choose your platform you choose your outcome, for better or worse. Besides, you can also use your experience to help other people. In the training course the following day there was a module on handling stress in the workplace. I was able to share the experience of the day as a real life lesson on the power to choose our response to things that happen in our lives.

No matter how often I clarify these Green Platform steps, there is the danger though of mistaking what I'm saying here for the real message.

"Feel the feeling fully, honour your human experience."

If someone close to you dies or if you lose a job or fail an exam, it is foolish to say in a cold, calculated way ... "it is as it is ... get over it ...get off your Red Platform" and do nothing further about it.

That kind of indifference or apathy would be as bad as over-the-top reacting without acceptance and positive action. It's a time for empathy.

"That's awful. You must feel gutted. Is there any way I can help you at this time? I'm here for you."

But not linear, logical, left-brain, cold, indifferent "it is as it is," with zero emotional intelligence.

If it's love, you honour the feeling. If it's an injustice you feel the anger but remember anger has no ethics. Anger is like a knife ... you can use it to stab someone or to cut someone free. Mother Teresa felt great anger when she saw the dying on the streets of Calcutta as people stepped over them on their way to and from their work.

She used the experience and the feelings arising from what she saw as a positive rather than a negative allowing it to eat her up inside. She channelled the anger into building the house for the dying so that no human being would ever have to die on the side of the street again where she lived.

She built that house and then built a thousand more bridges between the living and the dying so that people could leave this world with some sort of dignity.

You must honour your human situation. If you have two children who die in a car crash, it is essential that you honour all the grief, the anger, and the pain because real healing cannot take place without first of all experiencing and feeling fully that feeling.

There can be no healing without an authentic feeling.

The next step is to move out of the broken-ness and focus on well-ness. We need to stand in the darkness and proclaim the light, to focus on what we want, not what we don't want. We can only achieve one vision at the expense of the other vision. We have to choose a path or vision for the future ... a vision of broken-ness or well-ness.

Thankfully, these are extreme situations and mostly it is the day-to-day occurrences such as planes letting you down or losing an account in work that pre-occupy our thoughts.

If we are not careful though, the easy route when you hear that a customer has switched to a different company is to play the victim role.

Some time ago I was speaking at a seminar in the Sandymount Hotel in Dublin where I was talking on this very subject. One of the people attending the session not only didn't agree with what I was saying but also felt what I was espousing was very dangerous. This participant thought that I was in favour of repressing feelings and felt that these feelings might come out at a later time in a worse way.

I was delivering my presentation with slides, so I told him we would back up to the slide before the one where I showed the White Space clicking in and see the true sequence and steps of what happened after that.

He had become so caught up in the idea of hearing bad news and then accepting it coldly as 'it is as it is' that he had lost out on the part where I stressed how important it was to honour the feelings of loss or loneliness or regret. It's important to feel the human experience fully without someone accusing you of being on the Red Platform.

When we went back through the slides and the messages on each one again, it made perfect sense to him. I was glad he did it though – and told him and the rest of the audience as much. Why?

Because without that honouring of our emotions, it would be futile to just hear something terrible, and just accept it and move on. That isn't the human response. Who wants this kind of cold linear logical indifference and apathy in our lives? We are human beings not inhuman beings.

So I accept the situation and activate PAN: Positive Action Now. If I'm stuck in the swamp what good is it to anyone except the crocodile if I just bring acceptance to it and do nothing else? I must reach up to break a branch off the tree and use it to get out or call to someone passing by to throw me a rope. Of the 100 things that I could do, what is the one thing I can do now? Then do that one thing.

"What is the one thing that will improve this situation?" That's PAN. That's positive action now.

In retracing my encounter with the gentleman in Dublin, I also thought it would be apt to bring in something new to deepen his awareness of the "feeling fully" process. So I referred to the book,

'Tuesdays with Morrie'. This is a book Mitch Albom wrote about his dying friend and what it was like to die from a terrible disease.

However, in fact, the book was actually about living. Morrie would talk to him about various things in his life and often while doing so, he would feel pain. He would then say to Mitch, the author, "You feel it, you get into it, and then you detach from it."

"Detach," Morrie said again.

Morrie had nailed Step One of the Green and Red Platform process.

Morrie had discovered the great secret of life known to great philosophers, geneticists and healers... that the only way to conquer something is to get on the Green Platform and be one with it.

You cannot hate the pain, the fear, and the loneliness of The First Step before you step on the Red Platform and expect to beat it. Instead step on to the Green Platform and embrace it. Experience it. See it for what it is. Feel it. "Get into it," as Morrie said. Go through it and beyond it. Love it and then let it go. Detach from it and enter into the White Space. Now you have choices. Now you have "other emotions." Choose your platform. The emotions will follow. Positive on the Green Platform and negative on the Red Platform.

◆ When in fear, feel the fear fully, but choose courage, bravery and love on the Green Platform.

◆ When you're crying, cry the tears, but choose healing on the Green Platform.

◆ When you are standing in the darkness, proclaim the light.

◆ When in pain, feel it, see it for what it is, "get into it," then detach and choose freedom on the Green Platform.

◆ When you are angry, feel it, but choose harmony and inner peace on the Green Platform.

◆ When you are hurting, nurse yourself, but choose laughter and humour on the Green Platform.

◆ When you are exhausted, down and out, take it easy, rest, recover and choose freshness, creativity and contribution to others on the Green Platform.

It's truly transformational. When W. Mitchell (born William John Schiff III) bounced back from a variety of horrific accidents that left him wheelchair bound, he put this ability to choose your response succinctly: "It doesn't matter what happens to you, just what you do with what happens to you!"

So it's not what happens to you, your experiences, but the stories you tell yourself about what happens to you. Next we'll look at the power of our stories in our lives.

CHAPTER 6

The Impact Of Green Platform Stories

THE most magical words we've ever heard in our lives go back to our childhood when our parents tucked us into bed and all we wanted was a bedtime story.

"Once upon a time, long, long ago, deep in the dark forest, near a big river there was a magnificent castle, and in it lived a beautiful princess, but she was so sad. She was crying. Big tears running down her cheeks. Her heart was broken because she loved a poor woodcutter ..."

As humans, we are not hotwired for logic but we are hotwired for stories.

Your experiences in life have nothing to do with what is happening in your life, but everything to do with the meaning you attach to it. The story you tell yourself about your experience. How you experience what you experience is what matters.

Understanding this gives you a tremendous power to change the quality of your experiences, the quality of your results and the quality of your life.

The stories we tell ourselves are vital. In the Green Platform and Red Platform process we have the opening first steps. The first step is the human experience or the event. The situation as it is. You feel and experience it fully. Then the second step – the white space where we have the power to choose our responses.

This white space is vital to the quality of our lives because this space could also be called "story-telling" time or our "story-telling" space. Interpretation time. Decision time. Choosing my meaning time.

Facts have no meaning.

Events have no meaning.

A situation has no meaning.

To give an event meaning we must put an interpretation on it. In other words, we must make up a story about it. Is it a positive story on the Green Platform or is it a negative story on the Red Platform?

I'm the storyteller, I'm the author of my life, and so I can choose my story. Now the key storytelling question here in terms of our quality of life is this: "Why am I merely reacting to and making up a disempowering story that makes me feel bad while I focus on what I don't want to create and attract into my life on the Red Platform when I can just as easily choose my response and make up an empowering story where I focus on what I want to create and attract into my life on the Green Platform?"

Neither story has the power to change the situation or the event, but both stories have the power to radically change you into a victim on the Red Platform or a victor on the Green Platform.

By a 'story' then I mean those interpretations or meanings we create and tell ourselves and others that form the only reality we will ever know in this life.

It's your choice whether you are a passive reactive captive of your "poor me" negative Red Platform stories or a proactive captain of your positive uplifting stories on the Green Platform.

I can choose a disempowering meaning that makes me feel bad, or I can choose an empowering "opportunity" that makes me feel good.

When I choose the "disaster storyline" there is a septic tank of sabotage underneath the Red Platform waiting to trap me, disempower me and make me feel bad.

In contrast the empowering Green Platform opens up the field of all possibilities for me when I choose an "opportunity storyline."

John F. Kennedy was aware of the power of stories to deliver positive or negative energy. On the 12th of April 1959 he said, "Written in Chinese the word 'crisis' is composed of two characters – one represents danger and the other represents opportunity."

Is your glass half full or half empty? As Frederick Langbridge said: "Two men looked out through prison bars, one saw mud, the other stars." Different perspectives. Different meanings. Different stories. One depressing. The other uplifting.

We have millions of stories, opinions, meanings and thoughts about our families, our friends and co-workers, and most importantly, about ourselves. And the vast majority of our stories seem to be negative. We are generally victims.

We haul this sorry sack of mental baggage stories around with us everywhere we go. It accompanies us like the swarm of flies on a summer's day. Red Platform resentments, fears, anxieties, old wounds, losses, and regrets, as well as new worries of potential harms, and hurts in a fearful future. Our stressful thoughts are too numerous to list them all.

But we do have the power to empty that Red Platform mental sack of sorry stories and fill a new mental sack with Green Platform stories.

Perception is not just reality; it's much stronger than that. My interpretation or the story I tell myself has power and energy to shape my future and determine my destiny.

A story is our creation of a reality. Indeed, our story or our meaning or our interpretation matters more than what actually happens.

We live in the world our stories create. No matter how similar the situation or the experience, no two of us will create the same story. Feelings follow meanings. Feelings follow focus. Like the little ducklings following the mother duck down the stream, our feelings follow our stories. How I feel at any moment in time is the result of the meaning I've given to my experience, the story I tell myself. My story really does matter more than what actually happens.

You get a setback in life or in work.

You can hop on the Red Platform with your story: "This is terrible. This day is going from bad to worse!"

Or you can step on to the Green Platform: "I can handle this. These situations bring out the best in me."

I have my experience, yes, but the key experience is the thoughts I have about my experience, the story I tell myself about the experience.

My experience of my experience is what really counts. So it's vital to pay attention to what we pay attention to and how we pay attention. In other words, from which platform are we paying attention, the Green Platform or the Red Platform?

You have a car accident. The fact. The event. An accident.

"Bad things happen to me." That's the fabricated made-up story. This is the negative story or meaning with my feet firmly planted on the Red Platform.

On the other hand we have a choice. We can make up a positive energy-boosting story on the Green Platform:

"Thank God it was only the car. A hunk of steel or plastic. No one was injured and no one's feelings were hurt."

Some time ago when we had our visitor Sara from Denmark who told us a story about the night before she came to Ireland.

Someone stole her purse with her credit cards and all her other health cards, driving licence etc. in a restaurant. Upset, she phoned her Dad.

His response was a real Green Platform empowering story.

He said (she translated from the Danish): "That's fine, Sara. You're okay. You're all that matters. Those others are just dead things." (That was her direct English translation from Danish.)

What a marvellous response right off the Green Platform. "Those others are just dead things." Once he decided that the contents of her purse were just 'dead things', then there wasn't a big problem. Certainly not one big enough to upset a trip to Ireland.

What that incident brought home forcibly to me was the fact that we allow ourselves to create the story out of the reality we see in any situation. Indeed, our story or our meaning or our interpretation matters much more than what actually happens.

We end up living in the world our stories create. Sara's family didn't see the loss of her purse as a major issue. Yet I've seen people go into a flap and spend days and weeks upset when such a misfortune befalls them.

Which is better? To see a problem as a minor hiccup that can be overcome or to create a story where it's a major upset in you and your family's life.

The story you write for yourself in your head matters more than what actually has happened. It is never the event but the interpretation of the event that dictates your feelings.

Learning to detach and separate ourselves from our stories and look in on them, becoming the "Noticers," is an essential skill for creating our own piece of outrageous joy each day.

Rene Descartes wasn't aware of this when he said, "I think therefore I am."

He was wrong. I think it would have been more accurate if he said: "I observe myself thinking therefore I am." I am not the mental noise in my head. I can observe myself thinking and making up stories, but I am not my thoughts or my stories. I am the one behind the thoughts and stories, noticing them and making them up.

Understanding that you can choose the meaning you put to the events in your life gives a tremendous power to change the quality of experiences, the quality of results and the quality of life.

The most compelling story is the one we tell to ourselves about ourselves. That's why it's so crucial that our personal stories help us to build a positive self-image.

Telling stories helps us navigate our way through life because they provide structure and direction in the midst of the chaos of life. Stories organise and give context to the events of our lives as we experience them through our senses. Most of the time our senses make no sense anyway.

If I see a plane flying off into the sky, my senses tell me it's getting smaller and then it will disappear. Of course that's nonsense.

Our senses lie a lot of the time. The plane doesn't get smaller. It stays the same all the time.

But I say: "I definitely saw it getting smaller and smaller. In fact, it actually finally disappeared altogether." Not true.

Facts, events and situations are meaningless unless I create or manufacture a story around them. This is at the core of our happiness because again, we live in the world our stories create. Since we live in that world of our stories, it follows that a happier life comes from happier stories.

We continually create stories about what's happening in our lives. The reality we experience is completely subjective and we see it through our unique lenses and filters through which we view the world.

There are three major filters or lenses through which we view the world and make up our stories.

The first is generalisation.

The second is distortion.

The third is deletion.

These are more often than not Red Platform filters. But we can change them to Green Platform filters.

Such generalisations as: "What really annoys me is the way you always ..."

This then is the map for our story. We have just 'generalised' ourselves into an unhappy state.

My wife Annette once had a bad experience with birds when she was a teenager growing up in Queensland, Australia. Birds attacked her during their mating season. Ever since she is terrified of low flying birds. Even here in Ireland where the reality is that it's extremely rare to be attacked by a bird.

Try telling her that. Generalisations take over. We project past stories about experiences on to our current experiences.

So we continually make up stories about what is going on and what it all means, and no two of us create the same story.

On the other hand if Annette's first experiences with birds were happy ones, then the sight of a bird would elicit an entirely different story, and entirely different feeling, and an entirely different felt response.

Then we distort.

This is the second major filter. Send 10 people to see a show. You will get 10 very different versions of what happened. Each one will have a unique distortion.

Then the third filter... we delete.

Often we delete the good stuff so we land once again on the Red Platform.

You hear 10 positive things about yourself during the day and one negative thing. What are you thinking about on the way home from work? The negative. It's so easy to delete the positive.

I say to someone: "You're looking great, I love your hair and today you look really stunning, but what's wrong with your thumb?"

Ten years later I meet the person again. "Oh yeah, I'm the person that had the problem with my thumb." The rest, the good stuff is wiped out. Just press the delete button on any compliment.

It's hard for us, especially here in Ireland to take compliments. We either deny it or deflect it.

"That's a lovely dress you're wearing."

"Not at all, it's only an old rag of a thing."

People are much better in the US at taking compliments with gratitude.

"That's a lovely dress."

"Thank you so much, it's my favourite."

Or we deflect the compliment.

"That's a lovely dress.'

"Actually, I much prefer yours. Where did you get it?"

To be able to receive a compliment graciously and with genuine gratitude on The Green Platform is a great gift.

Then of course there are many other story filters of family, culture, county, religion and school or university that all shape our stories.

Frightening isn't it, to think that my reality is most of the time just my fabricated story. The stories we make up about our lives are just that – stories.

We create our life experiences through our thinking and story telling. It is not something that just happens to us. There's what happened in my life and then there's what I decide that it meant. It's my perception of events that cause how I feel. The meaning I put on it and feelings always follow meanings. It's not reality that causes us stress; it's our Red Platform perception which is at the root of how we feel.

And it's the same with joy on the Green Platform. When I was going to primary school in Ballinacree many moons ago our greatest joy was to play football in the school yard. Every break we would pick teams and then tear into a game for the 15 or 45-minute break.

One day an over-eager member of the opposition tripped me and I fell against a protruding stone in the wall and cut my forehead. I was "pumping blood." When I went into the school the infants' teacher saw me and straight away fainted.

Another student helped to clean me up and decided that day to become a nurse. Same situation. Two totally different responses. Two totally different stories. Two totally different interpretations.

One story drains energy. The other story gives energy. Our energy follows our stories. One person stayed connected to her joy on the Green Platform, and the other disconnected from her joy on the Red Platform.

Spiritual teacher Katie Byron is someone who really understands the positive and negative effect of stories. In her workshops she offers a gentle process of questioning our stories and beliefs. She invites you to be curious about everything – your relationships with family members, your ideas about illness and death, your feelings about your body, your worries about money, your anger at people who have hurt you and even your political allegiances.

Katie offers a simple process for inquiring into the true nature of reality, and especially into the things that feel distressing and upsetting. She calls her process "The Work."

The Work consists of four questions:

1. Is your story true?

2. Can you absolutely know that it's true?

3. How do you react, what happens, when you believe that story?

4. Who would you be without your (negative victim) story?

After answering the four questions, you go back through each one again and experiment with what Katie calls "turnarounds."

1. State the opposite of your story.

2. State the story as if the positions between you and your problem person were reversed.

3. Turn the story toward yourself, as if it is you that you are having the problem with, where you are the problem rather than the other person.

Turnarounds help you consider alternative perspectives that help reveal a truth you've been missing.

If you are on the Red Platform, then Katie's question can be life changing: "Who would you be without your victim story?"

Your Red Platform negative story is not your identity. It is not who you really are. You are not your story. Break free and try a new empowering story.

In Katie's process trying on new stories is like trying on new clothes, when we were comfortable in the old ones. When our default home is the Red Platform, it can be quite challenging to switch to the Green Platform even if we can create new hopes and new dreams and ultimately a new self-image.

You're essentially trying on different ways of thinking and talking to yourself about your life events and the people involved to see if the painful Red Platform perspective you've been holding on to could be jettisoned in favour of a truer viewpoint, one that feels good.

By walking a mile with new and different stories, you may find a new spring in your step, a new joy in your heart. Green Platform stories give you a way to live fully in the present by loving what is, by greeting each and every life event with curiosity and openness, instead of fear and anxiety.

Our stories may or may not conform to the real world. They may or may not inspire us to take hope-filled action to better our lives on the Green Platform. They may or may not take us to where we ultimately want to go. But since our destiny and our energy follow our stories, it is imperative that we do everything in our power to get our stories right, and get them firmly on the Green Platform.

Our bodies tell their own story. We are good at interpreting some of our body story lines such as when we see a smile or frown on a face. Similarly if we see someone with their shoulders thrust back in confidence or slumped roundly in despair, it is easy to detect the story line the body is sending out.

Even the way we walk tells a story – be it a liveliness or fatigue in the step. Our eyes too can show the sparkle of hope and joy or the blank misery of a sad stare.

As we walk and talk, our body language and our tone of voice give a clear understanding of the kind of thoughts that are in command of our bodies. Ninety three per cent of the impact you make on people when you walk into a room to give a presentation comes from your body language and tone of voice. Only seven per cent are the words.

Anything that uses up our energy is a story even if we don't call it a story. Earl Woods, Tiger's father and coach taught his son, that in every professional round there would be at least one troublesome shot, in deep rough, behind a tree, or buried in a bunker. Most of us would go into reactive mode, with quite a bit of bad language and tell ourselves a very disempowering story. We would normally go into default mode, react and land on the Red Platform.

Knowing that this scenario would happen repeatedly in golf,

Earl gave Tiger a very simple story in the form of a question to ask himself each time this happened.

Now instead of Tiger going automatic and reactive on the Red Platform with the typical negative story, Earl gave Tiger a "pre-cooked" positive empowering story to use. The little Green Platform story he gave Tiger was in the form or a question: "How will I hit this shot so brilliantly it will forever go down in the annals of golf?"

What an empowering story to implant in the young Tiger's mind. Sure enough in later years this story or meaning enabled him to hit those amazing shots.

For Tiger such moments weren't obstacles but opportunities. Not stumbling blocks but stepping-stones. Tiger was taught to consider that every problem he would face is there for one reason – to make him better.

Now I know a huge amount of personal troubles has fallen on top of his head some time ago. His wife and himself have split up and he has limited access to his two children.

For the millions of Dads or Mums who find themselves in that situation after a break-up, this represents a real stumbling block in their lives. I don't know how it will end up for him but I must say I was very impressed with his attitude to what had happened when he spoke to the media after therapy: "It's not what we achieve in life that matters, it's what we overcome," he said as he explained how he hoped to cope after the much-publicised break-up.

Indeed. "It's what we overcome," that really matters.

If he can live by that, then he is on the right road to becoming a better person. Being a better golfer depends on a number of factors but there is no doubt that he has arrested the slide down the rankings and is threatening something like the form which made him peerless for about a decade before his injuries and his private life took their toll on him.

From his father's early lesson and his own life-lesson, one

thing I think we can say about Tiger is that he understands the importance of the story he tells himself about the situation he is in. When you think of it, our capacity to tell stories is just about our profoundest gift in life.

For instance I knew a person who hated having to make weekly presentations in his work. Then he read Jack Black's MindStore where the author said that he made himself not only stop the fear of speaking in public but to convince himself that he was going to enjoy it.

I went to see him in Dublin a while back in the National Concert Hall and he recounted that very story. Jack had changed a thing he hated doing by rewriting his story.

Not only that, but he turned it into a way of making a living. That's the ultimate example of how you change your life around and make it pay. And be happier as well.

So this presents us with two challenges:

◆ To recognise how stories dominate our lives.

◆ To edit or rewrite our stories to get us on to the Green Platform.

For most of us, we have to become serious editors and do some serious editing. To edit a dysfunctional Red Platform story, you must first identify it.

To do that you must first ask the question: "In which important areas of my life is it clear that I cannot achieve my goals with the story that I've got?"

The 'perpetual victim' Red Platform story won't do that for us. Then we become the dreaded Red Platform 'Energy Vampires.'

What story and what energy are you bringing to the table?

Some people are very attached to telling themselves stories that make them "perpetual victims." You hear them always complaining. They latch onto all the bad news in life. My car engine blew up; my washing machine is going to cost me so much for a new part ...etc. etc.

If they don't know at this stage that from time to time engines do blow up or washing machines need new parts or burn out from years of use, then they are not really in touch with life as it unfolds, are they?

It has always been thus. Giving a bad story energy catapults you directly onto the Red Platform from where you are going to affect others around you with your negativity.

The ripples go out, one negative story begetting another one and that one in turn becoming a magnetic vibrational match attracting yet another one.

A negative story is like an open pot of jam on a summer's day attracting flies to it. That's why we should never underestimate the guile of the Ego to get us back on the Red Platform and 'enjoying' our misery. From the story of the car not working, the victim will follow on by telling his colleagues how much a replacement will cost and then how much those garage people will want for their labour and expertise to replace the engine.

By the time he's finished, we just tuned in to a soap opera where he is starring as the victim. If we hear enough of those stories in our lives, we begin to think there is no other way. Subliminally, we accept that we all are victims because these things happen to us all from time to time.

Tell the wrong, victim-laden story and I'm draining myself (and possibly those around me) of vital energy. Again, the choice is clear. I can tell myself a feel-bad story and anchor myself firmly on the Red Platform or I can choose to tell myself a feel-good story and immediately feel an empowerment on the Green Platform.

Is my story and my story's energy getting me 'busy dying or busy living' as Morgan Freeman (who played the character Red in the movie) famously remarked in the film 'Shawshank Redemption'? If we want to 'get busy living', then it is time to shut out all those negative stories that drain the energy from our day. Your story, which dies if deprived of energy, is not about death, but life. Not about the Red Platform but the Green Platform.

Yet if you continue to tell a bad 'perpetual victim' Red Platform story, if you continue to give energy to a bad story, then you will almost assuredly beget another bad one. You'll create that vibrational match where the feeling your story generates attracts more negative stories and more vibrational energy matches into your life.

The build-up of plaque in the arteries caused by poor diet is almost impossible to recognise at the time; we eat unhealthily, but we are unable to detect any immediate negative consequences, certainly not from one given meal, no matter how unhealthy. It's almost as if we got away with it.

You might rightly say that we are all entitled to a few negative thoughts from time to time. In the same way that a few greasy burgers won't affect our health there and then, we know that if we eat too many of them, they will mount up in our arteries and cause serious medical problems some time in our lives.

It's the same with a few negative thoughts. It's almost as if they don't matter. But as we continue to use them, they mount up in our lives. It's like the boiling frog syndrome. Throw a frog into a pot of boiling water and immediately he'll spring out. But if you gradually raise the temperature, and the frog in the pot doesn't recognise the gradual rise in temperature, he can't detect the danger he's in until it's too late and he's cooked and very dead.

The same holds true for negative story telling. While we do it we can't sense the full impact it's having because it's a gradual build-up.

"It's not that bad," we conclude. The cumulative effect of our unhappy damaging stories will have tragic consequences on our health, happiness, work engagement and performance.

Because we can't confirm the damage our storytelling is wrecking on us internally, we disregard it or ignore our gut instinct to make a change. Then one day we wake up to the fact that we've become cynical, sarcastic, negative and angry. How could we end up like this? Our default position and energy is on the Red Platform.

That's now who we are in danger of becoming.

Though we never quite saw it coming, that's now our story. We are firmly planted on the Red Platform with its powerful ABCs of anger, blame and complain.

It's quite amazing to discover that the key to all our problems, and fundamental to poor energy management, is draining storytelling on the Red Platform ... because it's storytelling that drives the way we gather and spend our energy.

It's the stories, again not the stories other people tell us, but the ones we tell ourselves that determine nothing less than our personal and professional destinies and our happiness or our unhappiness.

Tell yourself the right Green Platform story, the rightness of which only you can determine, only you can really feel – and the dynamics of your energy will change.

If you're finally living the story you want, it shouldn't and won't be an ordinary one. It can and will be extraordinary. After all you're not just the author of the story, but also the main character, the hero on the Green Platform. Keep challenging yourself with your stories to be the best that you can be, but make sure your goals are stretching but realistic.

Awareness is power, but it only becomes transforming power when it is full of compassion. When you become aware of yourself telling yourself a faulty negative story, don't go judgmental ... go compassionate, and gently replace your negative story with a positive one.

There's a huge difference between self-belief on the Green Platform and a false confidence that's out of touch with reality on the Red Platform. Self-delusion will never lead to self-improvement.

One man asked me on a course recently: "What's the difference between a positive story on the Green Platform and what he called 'spin?'"

Spin is based on self-delusion. A positive story on the Green Platform is not going out to the garden, seeing all those weeds and saying to yourself: " I must be positive, I must tell myself a positive story, 'There are no weeds.'"

That's spin. That's delusion. That's the kind of storytelling dressed up as a positive mental attitude that gives positive thinking a bad name. That kind of pseudo-positive thinking has to be named and shamed.

A positive story on the Green Platform is seeing the weeds and then having a vision of the garden in full bloom. Your next story is your plan, your strategy and your tactics to roll up your sleeves and work hard turning your vision into reality. A Green Platform positive story is based on honesty and rooted in reality.

If you're driving down the road and your fuel gauge is pointing definitively at "E," and you get a Smiley Face sticker and stick it over your fuel gauge saying, "All is well, I must be positive. I must tell myself a positive story."

That's "spin." That's delusion.

There are many television talent competition programmes where the young contestant's own opinion or their song or performance is solidly based on delusion.

"Well you're not a good judge and I'm going to be a famous singer no matter what you say."

Delusion. Spin. That stance puts you firmly on the Red Platform.

Again, awareness is power. There is enormous power in being aware, awake or alert. Get in the habit of challenging yourself on a constant basis about what is going on inside your head, and how your body is reacting towards those thoughts.

Why am I feeling like this? You know there are times when our systems are programmed to feel guilt or fear. Once you stop thoughts and ask yourself what is triggering this feeling, you will find that your awareness of such feelings will take away the worry.

This liberation of 'being aware' will be a wonderful transformation in your life if you continue to develop the compassionate "Noticer" inside. In this way, you will be able to rationalise why you were feeling the way you are and then put a stop to that daily draining of your energy. Simply by becoming compassionately aware.

Your Ego just wants you to go judgmental, to and be the "Negative Judgmental Noticer."

Then having noticed the negative story with compassion, go back on the Green Platform with an empowering story.

Let's go to the very worst range of bad story we face up to in our working lives – losing a job. It has happened to virtually all of us at some time or other. The trick in such an instance is the choice or interpretation we attach to that tough day in our lives.

Here's the typical negative Red Platform interpretation: "I can't believe they fired me. I worked hard here for 10 years. This is so unfair. They don't appreciate me. They've never appreciated me."

We are getting the typical story of frustration, which is understandable but will do absolutely nothing for that person except increase his sense of frustration, victimisation and unhappiness. There is an element of non-acceptance to it all. This person has decided to look at reality but interpret it with eyes of misery.

In this miserable drama, the person is writing a story that is becoming the real thing in his life. And he will continue to mistake his story for reality. But this person can change his view quickly by choosing a Green Platform interpretation. Say if he said something like: "Tough day but these things happen. I'm not the first person who has lost his job and I won't be the last one. Today is as it is."

Already we are seeing a very different interpretation on the story. Another story. Now he can add a truly positive interpretation by saying that really he had gone totally stale in that job and in a way losing his job would allow the person to do something really worthwhile. It would not just be a case of going through the motions to collect a wage at the end of each month.

In this instance, the person looks at reality and gives it a positive twist. Why not? It is much more uplifting that the alternative and will more likely lead to positive action to create a new job that connects to his purpose and makes his heart sing.

A question like: "How can I turn this into biggest opportunity of my life to really follow my dream?" can open up all kinds of new doors.

Since we are going to make up a story around this and every other situation anyway, it may as well be some interpretation or meaning that makes us feel good. It is important to recognise the difference between the facts of what happened and your story, your interpretation of what happened.

And we do this interpretation dance continually through the day. Go for positive Green Platform interpretations that make you feel good.

Your happiness, your positive emotion or your sheer joy is your greatest gift to your family, your co-workers, your community and ultimately to the world. These story choices will keep you in a positive energy field no matter what the circumstances.

When I was explaining this to a friend earlier this year, he said, "I wish I'd known this 20 years ago."

"Well," I said, "the Chinese say that the very best time to plant a tree is 20 years ago. But the next best time to plant a tree is now. So start creating positive uplifting energy boosting stories on the Green Platform now."

Then for the past I gave him the following exercise. He said that just doing this exercise made a massive difference in his life.

Here it is:

1. Write about a negative event that happened in your life. Include all the facts and details you can remember.

2. Write out the objective facts of what happened. Not your interpretation, not your story.

3. Write out your negative interpretation of the situation, the negative meaning or story you made up about it. Now you're well and truly back on the Red Platform

4. Turn that negative story into a positive story of that situation. Feel the positive energy flowing through you as you release that unhappy story ... your reaction and non-acceptance of life as it is. Use your positive story on the Green Platform to accept, embrace and love what is.

Now this again will not change the past situation, but it will change you, and give you a very important tool to create positive stories on the Green Platform. How can we use the Green and Red Platform to handle failure or setbacks?

I fail at something. I can land on the Red Platform (instantly lower my self-esteem) and tell myself a disempowering story that I am a failure. "I'm a total failure. I'm a disgrace."

Or I can tell myself an empowering story on the Green Platform. "There is no such thing as failure, only feedback. I am certainly not my behaviour. Failure is only the fuel to get it right next time. Rather than failure there is just only outcomes and results. A mistake is vile ... V.I.L.E. ... a very interesting learning experience. Now with my feedback and the lessons I've learned, watch me next time."

Next time thinking on the Green Platform is the key to bouncing back from failure. Create the gap that helps you see the vision of excellence for next time, and then ask the three Green Platform empowering questions:

◆ What can I learn from this?
◆ How can I grow from it?
◆ How can I serve humanity with the lessons that I've learned?

Then wring out your mistake or failure like an old dishcloth and fling it away. Once you've learned the lessons, the negative past is just a backpack filled with manure. Don't start telling yourself negative stories about it. Social media is a great modern tool today to help people to connect with each other. In itself it's neutral. But look how people use it to tell stories.

Some people see it as an extension of their Red Platform world and they use it to cyber-bully in toxic tweets and postings. The tragic result of this Red Platform activity can end up with teenage suicides that leave a trail of unnecessary pain for years and years.

Others use it to empower and build others up to their own life on the Green Platform. In this context, stories are inspirational and transformational. There's a huge need to get the social media generation telling their stories, tweets and postings from their positive position on the Green Platform.

One place where we find lots of Red Platform stories is in the whole world of worry.

Let's take a look at worry. The word worry comes from an Old English word that means to strangle or to choke. People literally worry themselves to death, or to heart disease, or to ulcers or high blood pressure or other nasty bodily conditions with their toxic stories on the Red Platform.

Forty per cent of the worry stories in our heads never happen.

Churchill said that most of what he worried about during the war never happened.

Thirty per cent we can't do anything about anyway.

"I'm going on a picnic on Saturday. I'm worried about the weather." The weather will be the weather. You can change your inner weather, but not your outer weather.

Twelve per cent are to do with the affairs of others that really don't concern us anyway.

Ten per cent are what the researchers call "petty and miscellaneous worries about health, real or imagined."

I met a woman last January. She said, "there's an awful 'flu going around. I normally get those thing." Two days later she had the 'flu. It was like the circus. If it was in town, she was not going to miss it. So 92 per cent of our worries are a waste of good Green Platform mental space on the Red Platform

Then eight per cent are genuine worry stories. These are a call to action on the Green Platform. Action and worry cannot co-exist. You cannot take action and worry at the same time. Just as light and darkness cannot co-exist and negativity and gratitude cannot co-exist.

If the roof is leaking call the plumber. If the brakes are dodgy on your car, bring it to a garage. Take immediate and decisive action and zap your worry in the bud.

But if you really want to worry, go to bed at night and fill your head with worst-case scenarios from the Red Platform. You can even get your foot shaking with the anxiety you'll create. But don't do anything or you won't be able to worry. Even having a notepad by your bed where you can list the things you can do, will catapult you on to the Green Platform.

Confront the worries directly on the Red Platform.

Put yourself sitting on a chair and imagine you are talking to yourself. Then imagine the worst thing that could happen. Prepare yourself mentally to accept the worst if necessary.

Then calmly slip off the Red Platform and take positive action to improve on the worst (which you've already decided to accept anyway) and then, hey presto, you're off. It's never as bad as you thought, is it?

Now decide to do something and you're back on an upward spiral. You'll get momentum. When you are pushing a bus, the first few yards are always the hardest. It gets easier as you get the bus rolling along.

Nowhere is positive story-telling on the Green Platform more powerful than in the whole area of forgiveness. And nowhere is the power of negative story telling on the Red Platform more destructive.

I bumped into a schoolteacher friend some time ago and I could tell from her body language that she was sad and full of misery.

"My husband left me," she explained.

"Can you forgive him?" I asked, taking her aback with my question.

"Of course not," was her exact answer, "I've too much respect for myself ever to do that." A pure Red Platform story.

"Ok, but remember when you are not forgiving him, you are telling yourself a negative story that makes you feel bad. In the meantime, he's out having a glass of wine or playing golf and probably enjoying himself," I said.

Forgiveness is the most selfish thing you can do in the best possible sense of the word. There's a huge difference between really loving yourself and taking care of yourself and being "selfish."

Not forgiving him is "like holding a red-hot coal in your hand intending to throw it at him but never actually getting around to throwing it," as the Buddha, Gautama Siddhartha put it.

Not forgiving is like drinking rat poison yourself and then hoping that the rat will die.

I then told my teacher friend about a Dublin woman who had a very abusive partner. She left him. Her friend asked her the same questions: "Can you forgive him?"

"Of course I can," she replied, "there's no way I'm going to have him living rent-free in my head."

She had found a place of inner peace on the Green Platform. She refused to blame him for putting her on the Red Platform. She took responsibility with her story.

If you've been hurt or betrayed in the past, by all means look for justice. By all means don't turn into a doormat, but even more importantly don't carry resentments around inside you. Forgive and move on. As Mark Twain said so graphically: "Forgiveness is the fragrance the violet sheds on the heel that has crushed it."

You have a choice of story here: To forgive and find freedom on the Green Platform or not to forgive and hang on to resentments on the Red Platform.

As the old saying goes: "You cannot prevent the birds of sorrow from flying over your head, but you can prevent them from building nests in your hair."

Forgiveness on the Green Platform is both powerful and

transformational and you end up feeling the better of it. Try it this week with someone you know falls into that category in your life.

Story telling is now a huge part of business.

Rolf Jensen of the Copenhagen Institute for Future Studies puts it like this: "We are in the twilight of a society based on data.

As information and intelligence become the domain of computers, society will place more value on the one human ability that cannot be automated: Emotion. "

Dan Pink is on a similar "power of story" wavelength in his book, A Whole New Mind: "The past few decades have belonged to a certain kind of person with a certain kind of mind – computer programmers who could crank code, lawyers who could craft contracts, MBAs who could crunch numbers.

But the keys to the kingdom are changing hands.

The future belongs to a very different kind of person with a very different kind of mind – creators and empathisers, pattern recognisers and meaning makers.

These people – artists, inventors, designers, storytellers, caregivers, consolers, big picture thinkers – will now reap society's richest rewards and share its greatest joys."

Whether in business or in your personal life, your ability to tell a story and communicate with yourself and others in a way that inspires positive action will be crucial in the coming years.

The whole world of advertising understood this a long, long time ago, and they still do. Story telling is at the core of all marketing.

So you see that whatever outcome you want to achieve in your life, the quality of the stories you tell yourself are central to it. These affect the quality of your life. Negative stories on the Red Platform will drain your energy. Positive stories on the Green Platform will boost your energy. Either way the is-ness or the "it is as it is" of the situation is a given. Your choice of story and your choice of platform will make all the difference.

Now we'll look at how one person changed her story and transformed her life in the process.

CHAPTER 7

Power Of The Right Story

THE real myth in our lives is that we have to feel bad first before something can change for the better; that we can only grow and change through suffering on the Red Platform. We can grow just as easily through joy and happiness on the Green Platform.

Negative emotions often block us from acting wisely and they also block our mental ability to determine right from wrong decisions.

When we are angry or frustrated – and most of us feel one or other of those emotions every day – we are allowing reactions that are not well thought through to take over our actions.

We are instinctively reacting out of pain rather than taking inspired action in a meaningful way. There is an enormous difference between moving from what we don't want to do and advancing in the direction of what we want to do.

Mostly the only thing missing from such a situation is you. Or the part of you that decides to bring acceptance to some situation or other and use that with a sense of joy as a springboard for positive action.

You don't live in the real world if you get up every day and expect a problem-free 16 or 18 hours ahead of you before going to sleep again.

In life we face brick walls. Their only purpose is to test us to see how badly we really want something or other.

Brick walls are there to be burst through. If you feed yourself an energy-laden story, then no brick walls is safe in your company.

If you take on a Red Platform story and you have no choice but to throw in the towel. To admit defeat. To say that nothing ever goes your way. Then the dream-killing dragon is more a friend of yours than you think.

The Green Platform is about breakthroughs. Success comes in 'cans' not in 'cannots.' When you empower yourself by declaring that you 'can' do something, you are writing a different story and interpretation for yourself which will help you take on the task with a greater sense of happiness or joy.

Always ask yourself: "Am I focusing on what I want or what I don't want? Where is my attention and energy going?"

A few years ago I met a woman in the United States who was distraught and unhappy because her boyfriend had just walked out on her. She was dropped like the proverbial hot potato. Carrie (not her real name) was virtually inconsolable – all teary-eyed and very, very upset.

She woke up one morning to find him packing his bags. When he saw her looking at him, almost nonchalantly he told her their relationship was over and he was moving out.

Despite her protestations, he didn't give her any further explanation. What's more he made it clear that he didn't want any further contact. That's a pretty raw state to be left in by any standards of relationship fall-outs.

This is when life is raw and real. I would have been crazy if I told her to make the best of it and enjoy the experience. That would have been foolish and without any foundation in the reality of her situation.

I told her that she had begun to do the right thing by crying and feeling the hurt, pain and grief of her broken relationship. I said that by doing that, she was honouring her feelings. Feeling the pain fully. Any healing has to emerge from a real and genuine feeling.

Then I added a rider, even as she cried in telling me the story. I stressed to her that while it was good to grieve at this time of loss, at the same time she should stop telling herself negative stories about what happened.

"If you continue to blame yourself or him or if you see yourself as a victim, then you will prolong and deepen the pain that you are feeling, " I explained.

I knew that wouldn't go down too well but it was important for her recovery that I planted the idea for her to consider. She sighed, a big, long sigh and said wearily: "What's positive about my story? You don't know how I'm feeling. I can't help the way I feel, and right now I'm seeing and thinking of only how sad my life is."

As this was one of the most real situations she would face in her life, the last thing I wanted to do was to be glib or formulaic driven in my approach.

I told her she was right.

I could only guess at the pain she was feeling and that was why I had mentioned that she should indeed honour her feelings. I made it clear that I wanted her to continue doing that.

And then I used the word 'but,' in a positive manner.

I told her after my 'but' I had something that would help her through her harrowing experience. I asked her if she thought it would be possible to think about controlling her thoughts? Maybe not straight away – but after a certain period of time.

Not unexpectedly, she wasn't jumping up and down full of enthusiasm with this suggestion but showed more interest when I put forward a possible technique. I pointed out gently to her how changing her thoughts would work. It's an old saying, I said, but 'change the way you look at things, and the things you look at change.'

I reminded her of Helen Keller's great remark as well, where she reminds us that often when one door closes in our lives, we should not spend so much time looking at the closed door that we can't see that another door is opening up for us.

I asked 'Carrie' to be aware that she had the power to change how she felt within herself. That was all I tried to get across to her.

I was leaving the US the following day and reminded her that in life feelings follow your thoughts. I asked that she should try to think of events and occasions in her life that had made her happy. People, sounds, feeling, places. "You won't be able to do it all the time but try it in short bursts," I suggested.

"That way, you will feel a little more energy and begin to start your recovery from the terrible grief you're now feeling."

When I was back in Ireland, there were times her sad face would enter my mind and I would wonder how she was coping through her break-up.

When I was back across the Atlantic the next time, we had a busy first four-day schedule which meant it was late in the week before I met her in the corridor.

I could see straight away that she was in a much better place than the tearful, let-down girl I had talked to the last time.

She greeted me with a big smile. One of happiness.

"Well, well," I said. "This is indeed a big change."

She brought me up to date. After I had gone back to Ireland, she said she suffered for days like she had never suffered before. The pain was so bad that she thought she would die. "But," she smiled. "That 'but' you spoke of, where you asked me to control my thoughts which in turn would help control how I felt. I did that and while it didn't turn off the sorrow, it lessened the flow."

"I also recalled the thing you said about the door from Helen Keller. Both those points stuck in my mind and as I became more and more conscious of them, I began to see that I could actually get over this."

As the days went by and a second week passed, she began to see that in the relationship she had been forced to give up a lot of personal goals and now she could think about revisiting those.

"So," I said teasingly, "and that is the sole reason there is such a huge smile on your face?"

She laughed out loud.

"No," she confided, "there is another reason. "

She had "just by chance, the most amazing coincidence" met a fantastic man and she was heading off to see him that evening.

I could tell she was energised in this new fledgling relationship. She was effervescent in her thoughts, words and actions.

She explained that her new man had an appreciation for her

and her goals that wasn't there with her previous partner. She felt more "free to be myself" in her new relationship.

It is indeed a strange world.

If I had dared to tell her the possibility of such an outcome a few months before when we spoke during her break-up, she would have told me to take a long walk off a short pier somewhere. And rightly so.

Sometimes it's hard in the middle of a crisis or trauma to see that it really does contain the seeds of a greater benefit and a better result in the long run.

So many times I've seen people devastated by the diagnosis of cancer, only to hear from them three years later that it was the best thing that ever happened to them, because they now had a much deeper and better connection with life, family, friends and what really mattered.

So with a little time and a little more perspective, 'Carrie' worked her way into a new and much better place.

She did so because she was brave enough to get off the Red Platform of victimhood and accept that – through all the pain – she could step on to the Green Platform and change how she thought and consequently how she felt.

Was it a coincidence or did she just re-programme her transmission signals when she moved from Red to Green Platform? We are all made up of little waves of information and energy. We're like transmission towers broadcasting on different frequencies. How do we change frequencies like a radio from FM 98 to FM 88? We change with our feelings. Then we get a vibrational match and we attract more of that feeling frequency into our lives.

Misery attracts more misery on the Red Platform.

Worry attracts more worry on the Red Platform.

Fear attracts more fear on the Red Platform.

Joy attracts more joy on the Green Platform.

Happiness attracts more happiness on the Green Platform.

Freedom attracts more freedom on the Green Platform.

When we change our feelings we change our frequency. To change our feelings we change our thoughts.

When you change your internal story, your energy follows, you get a different vibrational match and you attract and chart a new and better route through life. You manifest different things in your life.

How do you know that you are on the Red Platform broadcasting on a negative frequency and attracting more negative things into your life?

If you are feeling bored, hurt, worried, confused, frustrated, resentful, lonely, angry, stressed out, overwhelmed, disappointed, guilty, shameful, sad, anxious or depressed – then there's a fair chance you are on the Red Platform broadcasting on the negative frequency and attracting more negative things and negative people into your life.

If, however, you are feeling enthusiastic, passionate, happy, joyful, loving, appreciative, focused, abundant, relaxed, rested, free, creative and flourishing – then there is a fair chance you are broadcasting on the positive frequency of the Green Platform where you will continue to attract more positive things and positive people into your life.

You are listening to your own inner drum, following your bliss, following your own true north on your inner compass, living your truth and actualising your potential. You are living an inspired life and you are inspiring others. These realities as we've seen are at the core of Green Platform living, where we find our truer, better selves. We are creators of our own greater, better lives.

On the Red Platform the signal you are sending out is: "What am I getting from the world?"

"On the Green Platform the signal you are sending out is: "What am I giving to the world? How can I contribute? How can I make a difference? How can I use my gifts in the service of humanity?"

John F. Kennedy understood this concept of changing platform frequencies and vibrations when he remembered what his old schoolmaster used to say: "Ask not what your country can do for you, but rather ask what you can do for your country?"

Or your family or your company?

And as the 'Carrie' example shows, sometimes what first looks like a real sadness becomes a liberating force in a person's life. You have the control to change the station from news to music. Change the way you look at things and the things you look at really do change. 'Carrie' changed her thoughts, her feelings and her frequency from the Red Platform to the Green Platform and attracted a new "listener" to her wavelength.

Changing your story can really transform your life. Another powerful tool of real transformation is to become aware of the questions you use in your daily life. Changing your questions from the Red Platform to the Green Platform can bring about massive and instant action and change in your life. Next we'll look at this empowering process.

CHAPTER 8

A Question Of Power Or Poison

"WHY me?"

"What else is going to go wrong?"

"Why do these things always happen to me?"

These are poison questions on the Red Platform.

If there is one thing certain about living our lives, it's that if I ask a disempowering question on the Red Platform, I'll get a disempowering answer. It's 100 per cent certain.

Let's see how you're certain to get a toxic answer when you ask a toxic question on the Red Platform.

Disempowering questions beget disempowering answers.

However if I go back to the white space where I find the freedom to choose, I can come up with Empowering Questions on the Green Platform

These come in the form of "How can I? or "What can I ...?

These are Power Questions.

"How can I turn this around and enjoy the process?"

"How can I ..." or "What can I?" are the three most powerful words in the English language because they imply action.

Here are some Power Questions from the Green Platform:

"How can we double our productivity and halve our time?"

"What can I do to make this situation better?"

"What am I committed to today?"

"How can I make someone a little bit happier today?"

"What am I grateful for today?"

"What is the one positive thing I can do to make this situation better?"

"How can I find joy in my life today and bring that joy to others?"

When you challenge your subconscious like that (and it loves a challenge), it will work 24/7 to come up with an answer, a strategy or a plan.

So let's look at some common situations or events that crop up in our daily lives, and see how the questions we ask can deliver such a different response depending on which platform we are standing when we ask the question.

NO SALE

Red Platform Poison Question:
"When will they ever give me a break?"
Green Platform Power Question:
"How can I better serve my customers?"

NO PROMOTION

Red Platform Poison Question:
"Why does this always happen to me?"
Green Platform Power Question:
"How can I add value to the company and our customers?"

YOUR CHILD STRUGGLING AT SCHOOL

Red Platform Poison Question:
"Why can't the teachers do better?"
Green Platform Power Question:
"How can I help him or her with their homework?"

PEOPLE NOT DOING THEIR JOBS

Red Platform Poison Question:
"Why aren't they motivated?"
Green Platform Power Question:
"How can I improve my coaching skills?"

Other great Green Platform Power Questions are:
"What's the most important thing we should be talking about here today?"

"What's the one area that if improved would make the biggest difference in our team?"

"If you were an outside person coming in and knowing what you now know about our team, what advice would you give us?"

"What is the one thing we can do to improve this situation?"

"What are the 20 per cent of my tasks that are delivering 80 per cent of my results?"

"What are my strengths and how am I using them today?"

"What is it that brings me fully alive on the Green Platform today?"

Red Platform Poison Questions will always use the pronouns "you," or "they," or "them," and are always in the blaming and complaining mode. Whereas the Green Platform Power Questions always use the pronoun "I" implying responsibility. "How can I?" "What can I?" questions again always imply action.

But don't get trapped in poison loops of negative "Why?" questions.

Normally our "Why ..." questions are negative. You can of course get a positive "Why?" question. I remember one of the technicians working on the editing suite one day said to me: "I keep asking myself "why?" but in a positive sense."

"Why am I so lucky?"

"I have a job I love. I have a loving wife. I have a fantastic family. Why am I so blessed?"

He had flipped his "why?" question on to the Green Platform.

Let's look again at that empowering Green Platform question that has to do with gratitude.

"What am I thankful for today?" Gratitude and negativity cannot co-exist, so, "what am I grateful for today?"

Before we enter a heavyweight face-off here between Empowering Green Platform Questions v Disempowering Red Platform Questions, let me offer you some facts about the globe we live in that shows us how lucky we are to inhabit this part of the world.

I know that's a big, general sweeping statement in itself but if you have bought this book, are able to read, are not in prison etc., then you are so far ahead of most of the people on this planet that already you have won the lottery.

I understand that often it doesn't feel like that as you get sucked in to the day-to-day world of trying to earn a living, run a household and raise a family.

Still, it is no harm every now and again to take stock and say what we are thankful for.

If you are free and healthy, you are very lucky in a world context. Let's do a little task here by shrinking that world to a population of exactly 100 people. Now if we hold onto the existing human ratios and proportions, our Global Village of 100 would be populated by:

◆ 57 Asians
◆ 21 Europeans
◆ 14 from the western hemisphere, both north and south
◆ 8 Africans

That's the geographic bit done. Now if we were to further break down the numbers, we would find that our village contained:

◆ 52 females
◆ 48 males
◆ 70 non-white
◆ 30 white

In addition six people would possess 59 per cent of the entire wealth and all six would be from the United States.

Now to the living conditions of the 100 village people. Of that number:

80 would dwell in substandard housing.

70 would be unable to read.

Half would suffer from malnutrition.

Only one person in our Global Village would have had a college education and only one would own a computer.

I used the Global Village ratios to bring home the point that there are hundreds of millions and probably several billion people worse off than we are.

In terms of human life, I am indeed blessed – hundreds of times more blessed that the one million people who will not survive this week in the world for one reason or another or the billion people who are hungry today in our world.

If I have never experienced the danger of a life or death battle, if I have never suffered by being imprisoned, if I have not felt the agony of torture or the pangs of starvation ... I am ahead of at least 500 million people in the world and probably many times more than that. If I have food in the fridge, clothes on my back, a roof overhead and a place to sleep ... believe it or not I am richer than 75 per cent of this world's population.

If I have money in the bank, in my wallet, and even a few euro or a few dollars as spare change in a dish someplace ... I am among the top eight per cent of the world's wealthy people.

Sometimes we need a bit of perspective like this just so that while we may rightly seek a little help in our daily lives, we understand that we are fortunate in many ways.

I am just highlighting this to remind us all that we should be grateful on the Green Platform rather than moaning on the Red Platform.

I, too, am one of those who must realise that while I have many hopes and wishes for ways and means to enhance my life, I also acknowledge that already I have a fair degree of blessings there as well.

Years ago in St Columban's College, Dalgan Park in Co Meath when we were in the seminary there was an incredibly holy man there called Fr Tom Kennedy. He was a kind of living Francis of Assisi right there in our midst. I remember the week after I came home from the Philippines I travelled from our home in Dungimmon in Cavan to Dalgan Park at the foot of the hill of Tara. The first man I met was Tom. He was now much older, and bent over.

"How are you Tom?" I said.

He looked up at me. His eyes sparkled. He had such a warm welcome in his handshake and he simply said: "Ah, Declan, it's hard at times to count all the ould blessings. I'm so thankful for everything."

I've never forgotten Fr Tom's greeting. His challenge was counting all the blessings and being grateful for them. He had found the Green Platform long before I'd even thought of it.

What I'm saying here is we can be more positive about who we are and what we want even before we engage in any Green Platform process we are learning about here.

The best way to get tuned in to the Green Platform is to start your day as you mean to go on. So first thing in the morning, in the shower, download that positive gratitude from your inner software. Start off with empowering questions:

"What are the small things I can do today that will make me happier and increase my joy?"

"What are the small things that I can do to make others happier and increase their joy?"

It's just one more deposit in your happiness bank account, and they all add up.

When you throw a question like that into your subconscious you give it a problem. Your subconscious just loves to work on that for you and come up with a solution.

Say, for instance, you want to take a little more exercise to lose those few pounds which have been persisting a bit too long on your hips.

Just throw in a question like: "How can I get fitter," and it will begin a process of finding an answer for you.

Then when it gives you the answer: "Walk to the shops instead of driving," or: "Cycle to work instead of taking the bus or train," or: "Park your car at the farthest part of the car-park," it is offering you instant solutions.

It may well provide you options of add-on pieces of information like always taking the stairs instead of the lift at work, but by and large, your subconscious has done its work for you. Now it hands it over to another side of your brain to see if you have the discipline to carry out its proposals.

I don't think the importance of inputting Green Platform Power Questions or empowering statements into you head every day can be overstated.

They turn on a better colour in your head – a 'Green for Go' colour that sets off other traffic lights on your daily road to the Green Platform.

For instance if you ask yourself positively: 'How can I turn this problem around and enjoy solving it?" it is a million miles away from your Red Platform mindset if you say: "Why am I always facing these problems? They seem to follow me around."

In that last sentence, you are making yourself a victim and you're throwing in the towel before the first bell is rung. You are instantly giving away your power as your attention goes deeper and deeper into the quicksand of your problems.

You empower yourself every day with your Green Platform attitude or you disempower yourself with your Red Platform attitude. It's like electricity. Everyone has it in their home, but you can take the power away if you take out the fuse. All the potential electricity in your house is useless because you don't allow it to come in by not using the fuse to continue the circuit and make it work.

In your head, your attitude is the fuse. Without a good attitude, you will not go forward and indeed may go backwards. With a good fuse in your head, you can light up your day instantly. Once you decide you can do something or tackle a problem and decide to enjoy the process, your day turns around. You empower yourself to the power of 70 times seven.

Try it now and see how easy it is to switch on the light. I've stood on both platforms through my life and I know on which one I've been the happier. (And it's not the Red one.) It works every time once we have the awareness to put the right fuse into our thoughts and turn them into a good Green Platform attitude for that particular day.

When you get up in the morning you go to the wardrobe and you choose you clothes for the day. It's much more important to choose your Green Platform attitude for the day. It will have a much bigger effect on the people you meet than your clothes.

I have found that three of the most empowering words in the English language are: 'How can I....?" They send a signal to your brain that not only are you about to do something, but you plan to do it successfully and enjoy the process.

Make those three words part of your day, every day and you find that they will have amazing power to instantly transport you to the Green Platform and change your life for the better.

We have already been introduced to empowering beliefs on the Green Platform and disempowering beliefs on the Red Platform by Henry Ford when he said that whether you believe you can or you believe you can't, either way you are probably right.

There's a great story about Henry. He was asked one day where he got the "T" for his first Model T car. Henry knew instinctively that incrementalism or gradual improvement is the enemy of innovation. He didn't want to develop a faster horse. He went for total innovation. He wanted to build a horseless carriage. And he wanted to build 100 horseless carriages on an assembly line. He attracted a myriad of Red Platform naysayers telling him, "You can't do that, Henry."

So where did he get the "T" for his Model T. When his first car rolled off the assembly line on October the 1st, 1908, he told them, "The 'T'? I just took the 'T' out of can't. Now start taking the "t" out of your can'ts." On the Green Platform we find empowering beliefs that inspire us to say: "Yes, I can," like Henry. Now we'll look at beliefs, both positive and negative.

CHAPTER 9

Why Believing Is Always The First Step

BELIEF is the vital precursor to performance. One of the biggest barriers to achieving our true potential is the plethora of negative limiting beliefs that we've gathered over the years in our minds.

A belief is an assumption. It's assuming something to be true, to be a fact. A belief is not caused – it is created by choice. A belief about something's existence is not the same as its existence.

A football match is not a belief. It is a fact. It has an existence. But saying that playing football is good for you or bad for you is a belief. It's our beliefs that cause us so much stress. These are the stories we have made up for ourselves over the years and now steadfastly believe.

Our beliefs about events help cause how we feel. And because most of us are unaware of them, we allow them to limit our potential all our lives. Beliefs change the way we think, feel and act. The greatest way you can sabotage your potential is to feed yourself negative limiting beliefs.

Here are some of the more common ones:

"I don't deserve to get this."

"I'm not good enough."

"If it hasn't happened by now, it never will."

"If you knew what I'm really like, you wouldn't want me."

"I don't know what I want."

"Better stop wanting. If you get your hopes up you'll get hurt."

The good news though is that we can change our beliefs about events in our past. This will not change the past, but it will change the way you live from today on.

For centuries and even for many decades in the last century, it was genuinely believed that it was impossible for man to run a sub four-minute mile.

Experts told the world it was a bridge too far for mankind. That was until a medical student by the name of Roger Bannister came along.

When the British athlete broke that magical four-minute mile in 1954 he didn't just break the mile barrier, he broke one of sport's greatest limiting beliefs. This was underlined by the fact that once Bannister had shown it was achievable, then several other runners broke it within the same year.

In a way, Roger gave the rest permission and since then over 30,000 athletes have broken a standard which it was thought would never happen.

In fact, Eamonn Coghlan pushed the concept of breaking it even further. The great Chairman of the Boards in the US and now a Senator in the Republic of Ireland, became the first man to break it as a 40-year-old.

He believed just like Roger. Both knew that belief comes before performance. Your beliefs are how you create reality. In fact in 1999, Hicham El Guerrouj ran the mile in 3.43.13 minutes knocking nearly 17 seconds off the famous four-minute mile.

In 1940 an Afro-American girl was born prematurely. Somehow she survived. Then she got double pneumonia but again she survived.

Then scarlet fever. Survived that too.

At age six she contracted polio and was confined to a wheelchair and the doctors said she'd never walk again.

One day as she was looking out through the screen door at her brothers and sisters playing basketball, she began to cry.

"I want to be out there playing basketball but here I am stuck in this wheelchair for the rest of my life," she protested.

Her mother challenged her straight away.

"Who are you going to believe? Those doctors or me, your mother? Starting right here, right now we'll get you out of that wheelchair."

So she did.

At 11, she got out of the wheelchair.

At 12, she got rid of the leg-braces.

At 13, she played basketball with her brothers and sisters.

At 14, she started to run.

At 15, she started to run fast.

At 16, she started to run very fast.

And four years later, at 20, she was the fastest woman on the planet with three gold medals from the 1960 Olympics in Rome. That's the story in abbreviated form of the great Wilma Rudolph.

That's belief.

The you you see is definitely the you you'll be. You can see a wheelchair or you can see Olympic gold.

Most of our wheelchairs are mental. Inside. Limiting our beliefs.

Belief comes before performance.

To achieve your potential, to achieve performance, alter your belief.

When Liam Griffin won the All Ireland hurling final with Wexford in 1996 he spent a huge amount of time in not just building up belief within the team, but also creating the stuff of legends with the stories of how he broke limiting beliefs within the players.

He used every belief building block he could find from planting Wexford flags on the graveyards of famous hurlers of the past to visits to holy islands to getting off the bus at the Wicklow border reminding them that the next time they crossed back over they would have the Liam McCarthy cup. He did anything he could think of to carve out and stack up the building blocks of belief, one by one.

The Clare legend and Dublin's hurling manager Anthony Daly has an Aladdin's cave full of stories about their All Ireland wins in the nineties and the steps Ger Loughnane took to break limiting beliefs including the toxic mythological curse of Biddy Early.

He told me recently that far from being a witch she was rather a great healing woman simply living in the wrong century.

Quite simply Ger replaced all the negative stuff with powerful new beliefs and delivered that first amazing Munster final and then two All-Ireland finals.

There's a massive 875km ultra-marathon down in Australia that goes from Sydney to Melbourne. One year a potato-farmer from the Otway hills appeared at the start wearing a pair of wellingtons or gumboots as they called them. His name was Cliff Young. He was 61 years old.

"Have you ever run a marathon before Cliff?"

"No."

"Half-marathon?"

"No."

"Cliff, did you ever run a race in your life?"

"No."

"Then why are you here?"

"Well, I was coming home from the pub the other night and I thought, wouldn't it be great to run from Sydney to Melbourne? Imagine telling the story to my mates in the pub."

The organisers thought he was cracked but they allowed him to chug off in his wellies thinking he'd only last an hour or so.

He knew he could drink and take toilet breaks on the way, but Cliff never ever heard of anyone going to bed during a race. The idea of running for 18 hours and sleeping for six never occurred to him.

So he just kept on shuffling along Forest Gump-like.

He ran at a slow loping pace and trailed the leaders for most of the first day, but by running while the others slept, he took the lead the first night and maintained it for the remainder of the race. They later called this the Cliff Young "shuffle."

Then on April 29, five days, 15 hours and four minutes after he started, Cliff ran into the Westfield Centre in Melbourne over 10 hours ahead of the field. He won the race. He was given $10,000.

He just broke it into five wads of $2000 and gave them out to the next five runners who came in after him.

Cliff broke a limiting belief.

When he was asked how he did it he said he just imagined he was running after sheep all day like he did when he was a young boy growing up on the farm. In that way he blocked out every negative thought and limiting belief. Cliff epitomised the words of John Stuart Mill, when he said: "One person with a belief is equal to 99 who have only interests."

Nikos Kazantzakis, who wrote Zorba the Greek, put it even better: "When you passionately believe in what doesn't exist, you create it."

We all create our own problems based on our beliefs. If you are a person with money problems, chances are you will always have money problems. It's as if you have a money set point and will squander anything that comes in above that.

You may not realise it but this is based on your beliefs.

The person with a relationship disorder will always have a relationship disorder. It's as though each person specialises in a disorder or malfunction. Beliefs, unconscious or not, are creating these events. Until the beliefs that are creating these events are recognised and let go, they will continue to recur.

If you look at your life, it is generally a direct result of your beliefs. Not happy? Bad health? Big debt? Some part of you, your beliefs, wants what you have, problems and all.

How do you change?

It starts with selecting what you want in your life. As soon as you select what you want to be, do or have you'll discover a huge amount of limiting beliefs that are in the way, stopping you. They'll surface to meet you. Most probably they are your excuses. In life, you either make excuses or make things happen. Pay attention to your complaints so that they become goals or intentions for you.

"What do I want?"

"What makes my heart sing?"

"What would I attempt if I knew I couldn't fail?

The key to life is where you focus. If you focus on what you want on the Green Platform you'll discover on that platform the beliefs that will make that happen.

If you focus on what you don't want, you'll discover those beliefs on the Red Platform that will make sure you won't ever get what you want.

Focus on lack and you'll get more of lack. If you focus on excuses you'll attract more excuses. You have to dig down deep to find the beliefs that are sabotaging your potential or to discover the beliefs that are helping you achieve your true potential.

As the Swiss psychologist Carl Jung said: "Until you make the unconscious conscious, it will direct your life and you will call it fate."

So whether you believe you can on the Green Platform or you believe you can't on the Red Platform, either way, you're probably right. One way or the other beliefs do, in fact, come before performance.

Ultimately beliefs determine how we use our energy and also determine whether we live in a friendly or an unfriendly universe.

CHAPTER 10

The Friendly Or Unfriendly Universe

THE great scientist and philosopher Albert Einstein once said that the key to life boils down to whether we believe we are living in a friendly or an unfriendly universe.

You can see why he was good on relativity.

In essence, he was asking us where do we focus and what do we see?

Life is either a series of problems or opportunities? Do we believe that the universe is out to do us good, or is it out to "get us?"

The answer to his riddle tells you if you are an optimist or a pessimist? If you see problems, you are right for you and if you see opportunities, you are equally right.

The pessimist too will build a body of sufficient evidence in the world around him or her to say that optimists are not living in the real world. How can anyone be optimistic if he or she has just lost his job and sees the whole scenario as a disaster?

Similarly the optimist will find enough evidence to prove his point. He or she will look on the end of his employment as the right time to re-assess his working life and face up to a new challenge.

Crucially though, he or she will enjoy a much better quality of life, since all negative thoughts weaken and dis-empower us and turn us into magnets attracting more negative stuff into our lives.

However the optimist will generate different, positive feelings by his or her attitude and this in turn will raise the vibrational frequency of consciousness to act and attract more positive things into their lives.

All medical research suggests that positive energy and positive thoughts are better for our physical health. Negative thoughts weaken our immune systems. The greatest single boost to our immune systems is laughter.

That lovely old Jesuit priest Pierre Teilhard de Chardin, who was gifted with both a compassionate heart and a brilliant mind, once said during a visit to China: "In the final analysis the question of why bad things happen to good people transmutes itself into some very different questions, no longer asking why something happened, but asking: 'How we will respond, and what do we intend to do now that it has happened?'"

Notice the key in Pierre's remark... "to do now."

A different question.

A different story or meaning.

And positive action.

Basically, he is telling us that feelings follow meanings. Feelings follow focus. How I feel right now depends on the meaning I've given to the situation.

I can either live in what I perceive to be a friendly or an unfriendly universe.

When bad things happen to good people you see a whole variety of different responses.

People become victims on the Red Platform or they become victors on the Green Platform. They turn into bitter people, disfigured people on the Red Platform or they develop and grow into better people, transfigured and transformed people on the Green Platform.

We had a terrible tragedy in Bray, Co Wicklow some years ago. A lovely young man, Seb Creane was stabbed to death in an incident that tore into the hearts of two families as the man who did the stabbing shortly afterwards fatally stabbed himself.

A few days later, Seb's mother, standing in a pool of grief, gave the eulogy at the funeral in the Holy Redeemer Church in Bray. It was packed with many young people as well as shattered relatives and friends.

First Nuala Creane took them into the white space and offered them a choice. Then (and I'm not sure if she was aware that there is such a thing as the Red Platform) she took them on to the Red Platform.

She gave them a victim-blaming view of life from the Red Platform.

Then she paused, and switched on to the Green Platform. She gave them a different view. A different story. A different meaning. A different interpretation.

Here's what she said: "And as a result we, my beloved Jay and I, and all of you, are faced with a choice:

"Do we continue to live in darkness, seeing only fear, anger, bitterness, resentment; blaming, bemoaning our loss, always looking backwards, blaming, blaming, blaming ... Or are we ready to transmute this negativity?

"Can we rise to the challenge with unconditional love, knowing that we were born on to this earth to grow? Our hearts are broken but maybe our hearts needed to be broken so that they could expand."

She got a prolonged ovation.

Old Fr. Pierre would have been proud of her:

"In the final analysis the question of why bad things happen to good people transmutes itself into some very different questions, no longer asking why something happened, but asking: 'How we will respond, and what do we intend to do now that it has happened.'"

As Viktor Frankl discovered in the death camps, the power to choose either Green and Red Platforms, the ability to choose still works, even when bad things happen to good people.

When we are faced by something that we cannot change, we are challenged to change ourselves. In Man's Search for Meaning Viktor says:

"We must never forget that we may also find meaning in life even when confronted with a hopeless situation, when facing a fate that cannot be changed. For what then matters is to bear witness to the uniquely human potential at its best, which is to transform a personal tragedy into a triumph, to turn one's predicament into a human achievement."

Nuala's gift was to show us precisely how to do that, no matter how painful the situation. She pointed the way onto the Green Platform even though reality pointed us all to the Red Platform.

She also taught us that you can be in enormous grief, and still live on the Green Platform feeling your grief fully and honouring the tearful situation. We can stand in darkness and still proclaim the light.

Is it possible to be born and live on the Green Platform?

It is. We'll meet him next.

CHAPTER ELEVEN

Meet Alexander The Greatest

OUR third child, Alexander, is a very special child. He was born with Mowat-Wilson syndrome in December 2004 and is severely mentally and physically disabled.

He has many difficulties. For instance he:

◆ Can't speak
◆ Can't walk
◆ Is peg tube-fed through his stomach
◆ Is doubly incontinent
◆ Suffers from life-threatening status epilepticus seizures
◆ Was in ICU on life support for two weeks a few years ago
◆ Suffers life-threatening allergies
◆ Has had one anaphylactic attack
◆ Has a metabolic disorder profile

Alexander requires round the clock nursing care. You could say he's been dealt a very tough hand of cards in life. But it's how he plays them that is special, not just for himself, but for all of us who live with or around him.

He was also born on the Green Platform. His mission in life is to teach us the essence of life there and to eschew the temptation to step on the negative Red Platform.

How can that be so, you may well ask? Well, for starters, he is unconditional love or at least as near as we'll ever get to it. He doesn't have an Ego, and because of that there is no magnetic false-self pulling him on to the Red Platform.

◆ He doesn't do the past.
◆ He doesn't do the future.
◆ He only does the present.
　Here.
　Now.

His simple message from the Green Platform is always the same:

Be here. Now. It is the essence of Zen.

You are only doing what you are doing.

I remember asking a Zen Buddhist monk one time in Japan what was Zen? He said: "Before enlightenment, chopping wood, drawing water? After enlightenment, chopping wood, drawing water! But oh, what a difference."

"Chopping wood, drawing water!"

If you are chopping wood, you are chopping wood; if you are drawing water, you are drawing water.

If you are Alexander, you're living in the now. As clear and as simple as that.

Not the mental noise of the thinking mind goaded into the future by the Ego that cannot live in the now with its victim stories: "How many more years will I have to chop this wood?"

No sign of a ledger relationship.

"Why do I always have to draw the water?"

"Why is it always me?"

Alexander invites us to be here, fully present. His presence keeps us fully alive, awake, aware and alert on the Green Platform.

As the Persian poet Rumi memorably said: "The future and the past veil God from you. Burn both of them with fire."

He was a Green Platform man from long ago and had that attitude in common with our Alexander who only exists in the here and now.

"Take no thought for tomorrow ..."

"Look at the flowers of the field how they bloom ..."

"Unless you become like little children ..."

Like Rumi, Alexander says to us: "Sell your cleverness and purchase bewilderment, awe and wonder."

Alexander's presence is always a signpost, teaching us, showing us and pointing us to another dimension of living.

The joy dimension.

The 'don't try so hard' dimension.

The 'be one with life' dimension.

The 'go with the flow of life' dimension.

Flowers bloom.

The sun shines.

There is no effort involved.

Alexander reminds us of that. Like the sun, all he wants to do is shine love into our lives even though the clouds of pain often cover his face.

Apart from those times when he is in pain, he is almost always smiling, waving and clapping his hands. A friend saw him on the seafront in Bray one time smiling and waving at every single passerby and he said to me: "Alex is like a little pontiff. It's as if he is blessing us all."

His mother, Annette is Australian and although we live in Ireland, she likes to go home every few years to meet up with her family and friends and give our children a sense of what Australia and their Australian heritage is all about. When her parents were alive this was one of her top priorities.

I was on a work tour in America some time ago when they went to Australia and Annette told me this amazing story on her return. She recalled how the plane had gone into severe turbulence for a part of the journey. It was a very scary experience. She described the turmoil as the plane dropped hundreds of feet in altitude. People were screaming all around.

Our eldest son Fionn (about 11 at the time) was being very manly and brave amid all the mayhem. Annette saw him put a protective arm around his older sister Genevieve (14) to re-assure her.

All the while Alexander, sitting beside his Mum, thought it was just great fun. Every time the plane dropped suddenly, he laughed with apparent delight and clapped his hands. For him, these were moments of outrageous joy. He was making different choices to all those around him. A different interpretation. A different meaning. A different inner story in his head.

Now I am not saying we should all feel happy if there appears to be such danger imminent in our lives. What I am underlining is the fact that life's only meaning is the one we decide to give it. Alexander didn't have an Ego feeding him a diet of fear.

Think about that for a while. If you normally worry about something, decide as an experiment tomorrow to enjoy the moment instead of losing the moment in worry.

In his state, he is not hard or tough. He is soft. But there is a huge strength in his softness. He reminds me of what the Tao Te Ching text said on this: "The softest thing in the universe overcomes the hardest thing in the universe."

The 'softest thing' referred to is water. We see how, in the course of time, water can erode rock; how, without trouble, it disappears into the earth. Water looks soft, but really is very strong. Because it is silent and unpretentious and seems to have 'no substance', it achieves its purpose.

He doesn't work hard at making friends. He just is as he is. That's enough. Magnetically he attracts friends.

As Dr Roisin Mulcahy from Bantry, Co Cork memorably put it: "Children with special needs like Alexander ... they soften the hard edges of society for the rest of us."

Alexander is not under time pressure. He's not currently working on his PhD., yet he's an extraordinary professor teaching us what real love is all about. He shows us that we are not what we do (our work, our job, our title.) He teaches us that who we are matters much more than what we do.

Nor are we what we have, or even what other people think of us, our reputation. It's who we are and who we become in his presence that matters.

When he looks at you and smiles, it's as if he's saying: "Give today your best shot and let fear and doubt go. Live out of unconditional love and freedom. Find joy today all around you."

Alexander is always in the precious present. He is the ultimate cure for destination addiction or outcome addiction.

He doesn't do all that Red Platform stuff.

He doesn't label.

He doesn't judge.

He doesn't evaluate you and then decide how he'll respond to you. He lives in the Green Platform unconditional love zone.

When Genevieve and Fionn, his brother and sister, were growing up, it was often in the world of action and doing.

"Brush your teeth."

"Do your homework."

"Tidy your room."

'Hurry up. Get ready."

"Put away the dishes."

"Come on. Let's go ... now.'

As you look at, listen, touch or help Alexander with this or that you join him in being completely present, not wanting anything other than the moment as it is. He helps transport all of us to a different place in life. The world of "being" behind all the "doing", A higher level of consciousness. Now there is nothing wrong with the doing, but if our lives are only about the "doing", and no time for "being", then our lives will be very impoverished. After being in his presence, then we can go back energised to the "doing" again.

That's how he enriches us all – his mother Annette, his sister Genevieve, his brother Fionn, Mary, his godmother, Hugh, his godfather and all who come into his presence.

Fionn has a special relationship with Alexander. Real brothers. They play for hours together like young wolves, nuzzling and rolling and having fun. Their laughter echoes through the house. It's like they're joined at the hip.

Sometimes he can be in pain. We all try to humour him but it doesn't work. Then Fionn walks into the room. Alexander's face lights up and the connection with his big brother transcends the pain he is feeling. It is something else to behold. Fionn can do for him what painkillers can't do. He has the gift of putting Alexander back in good humour within seconds. A little magic. Or maybe a little miracle.

Sometimes it can be exhausting minding Alexander through the night when he is in pain but there isn't a day that he doesn't give us something special back. Annette is the most enriched of us all because she gives him so much of her time, her love and her tenderness. When it comes to Alexander, she is totally altruistic. There are days and nights that she doesn't shut an eye minding him, yet there is always a sense with her that Alexander is a privilege she has been granted in life.

It is the highest form of love I've ever witnessed. All of us who live in Alexander's circle feel our own degree of privilege. The enrichment finds many expressions and pulls people on to the Green Platform.

Genevieve captured the whole Alexander effect on our household better than anyone as you will see from her poem below. One night years ago, she stayed up late writing. We didn't realise it at the time but she was putting her own views on the enrichment of knowing Alexander down on paper.

The next day she showed us her work. She had written a poem about her little brother, or as she playfully calls him Alexie Balexie Boo. She mentioned 'Fee-fon' in it, which was what she called our oldest son Fionn when she was young, as she couldn't get her tongue around saying Fionn. Here's her special poem:

MY ALEX

At three minutes to midnight on December the 10th,
You were new to the world and took your first breath,
A gentle baby boy with wide-set eyes,
They sparkle when you're happy and shine when you cry.
People often comment on your beautiful eyes,
their expressive colour, ever trusting, never shy.

You achieve what you do, you do what you can,

It's hard to perform with Mowat Wilson syndrome.
Yet the ability to love, to "live in the now," that's pretty rare, but you
know how.
Your happiness is special, the tint of your hair,
you've been sick a lot, and I'll always be there.
The sounds of your chuckles are laughed with great taste,
It's something I can't describe,
it's nothing I could paint.

Strangers are your friends, you stop, smile and wave,
What a beautiful little boy in that little walking frame.
My baby brother, Alexander,
I love you in every single way,
If it weren't for you, would I still be the same person I am today?
I love to hug you and keep you very close,
It's one of the things I love to do the most.
I'm proud to be your sister and also Fee-fon's too,
Our beautiful baby brother, Alexie Balexie Boo.

Not everyone has an Alexander to get them away for a while from the world of "doing" and into the world of "being." We are human "beings," not human "doings." Now we'll look at ways to access this world of "being."

CHAPTER 12

The Story Of 'Being' And 'Doing'

SO many of us just lay out our lives in a linear fashion and tell ourselves that's the way it is meant to be. We get up, we go to work, we exercise, relate to our families and slot all these activities into our day.

We are working hard to get through our day and if we 'get' our lives at that level only, then we are getting the quantity but missing the quality. Life is just one thing after another.

Here's a Green Platform question which will tell if you are bringing added value to your day: "When you are exercising, working or relating to your family ... are you also bringing joy, ease and light to these encounters or are you just ticking off a things-to-do list? Are you getting and bringing some happiness to your day or are you just getting through it? In other words, ask yourself – what am I like 'being' while I'm 'doing'?"

Life is hard right around the world at the moment with big cutbacks in public spending and a downturn in job opportunities as we try to raise our families and educate them. In fact, sometimes we feel it's a miracle in itself that we get through our day in one piece without having time for the "being" thing I'm speaking about.

Actually the "doing" and the "being" are linked in many ways. There is joy in the everyday, in the ordinary, by celebrating "the habitual and the banal" (to misquote slightly one of my favourite poets Patrick Kavanagh). "God is in the bits and pieces of Everyday. A kiss here and a laugh again, and sometimes tears ..."

Deep within us we have joy. It's there all the time. We never lose it. We just lose touch with it. We lose our connection to it. The real magic and fun in life is when you reconnect and bring those inner joyful forces to what you are doing from deep inside you. It goes back to that sense of awareness I keep mentioning which only comes when you stop all the noise in your head and come fully into the present on the Green Platform.

Once we do that and only hear the tick of the clock in the background and sense we are part of this universe right here, right now, it is a truly empowering feeling.

Tell you what. Let's drop what we are doing (unless you are holding a baby or something you obviously shouldn't drop), sit down and either focus on the wall opposite with your eyes open (if you are in work) or decide to close them if you are in a private place at work or are at home.

Once you become aware of the one who is observing everything, your "Noticer", real growth can take place. When you become aware of the present moment in this breathing meditation as you focus on the breath ... because the body is always in the present moment, then real transformation is possible.

So just close your eyes and follow the breath ... listen to the sound of your breath as you inhale and then as you exhale ... in ... and down ... and up and out ... in ... and down ... and up and out ... in ... and down ... and up and out ... in ... and down ... and up and out ... in ... and down ... and up and out ... in ... and down ... and up and out.

When thoughts or feelings or sensations come in, don't try not to think of them or don't try hard to put them away ... rather befriend them ... put them in the chair beside you ... find out what do they really need ... in a friendly relaxed manner ... acknowledge them, (don't try to banish them because what you resist will persist, what you battle against you create) and then gently back to the breath.

Gradually you move from the absence of thoughts and feelings to the presence of peace. This is what silence is really about ... the presence of peace. It's just there. So relaxing.

When the breath is the focus, the rest – the thoughts and the feelings will gradually fall off the table.

This type of meditation is a putting aside and an emptying of the Egoic Red Platform chattering mind, and gets you to experience the "Real You" on the Green Platform. It's creating that empty space where the observer and the observed can merge, where the lover and the beloved become one, where union happens.

Getting to it is like going through a paper wall. It's so easy you wonder why it has eluded you for so long. Yet it is totally energising, compared to the slavish energy-draining automatic unobserved compulsive living out of the mental noise in your head, that static that's so similar to radio reception interference.

Remember to breathe properly with none of the old 'chest out, stomach in' type of stuff you were taught as a child. That's the opposite of how you should breathe.

BREATHING PATTERNS

Very nervous	35 to 40 breaths per minute.
Nervous	20 to 28 breaths per minute.
Normal	12 to 18 breaths per minute.
Meditation	6 to 8 breaths per minute.

The correct way to breathe involves taking a deep breath, and filling the bottom of your lungs, rather than the upper chest. Just like a baby.

To test this, just put your hands on your hips, with your forefingers just about touching your navel ... your thumbs just resting on the hollow above each hip. Now taking a deep breath, just feel your abdomen swell beneath your fingers and thumbs. Concentrate on the bottom of your lungs as you inhale, and be careful not to move your shoulders. Now you have it.

◆ Thoughts ... gently place aside on the chair beside you.
◆ Feelings ... gently place aside on the chair.
◆ Sensations ... that twitch, just the same, gently on the chair

And then simply,
- Breathe slowly ...
- Breathe deeply ...
- And follow the breath. Listen to your breathing, about six to eight breaths per minute, and feel the deep peace.

Scientific studies that show the benefits of meditation:
- Blood pressure comes down.
- Stress is alleviated.
- Basal metabolic rate goes down.
- A number of psychosomatic disorders are relieved and disappear.
- There is increased brain wave coherence that improves attention span, creativity, learning ability and memory retrieval.
- The immune system is boosted.

You can do this for five minutes to begin with and then you can gradually get up to 10 or 15 minutes. Just stay with it and you'll feel so good afterwards that you'll really miss it if you stop doing it.

Then you can do the condensed version – the Green Platform 60-Second Time Out. It's like an ad break if you like.

If you are doing this for the first time, you will realise that as you breathe and follow the breath and listen beyond yourself in the room, out into the garden or road beside you, that there are several little sounds vying for your attention... a child crying, a bird singing, a clock ticking.

You can go with the thoughts at first and sail out over the trees into the field and then watch back down to earth as you allow your imagination and mind to soar, like a moon rocket, up into the atmosphere ... watching back at the little orbit, this little blue spinning planet where we make our home.

NASA's Saturn system probe snapped imagery of the Earth and Moon on July 19th, 2013. The Earth is a tiny, almost luminescent blue marble, a not-quite-so-pale blue dot. The camera taking the picture was 898 million miles away.

That's our galaxy. Now consider that there are 300 billion galaxies each with billions and billions of stars – then we can have some idea of our place in this awesome universe.

But then back to the breath.

It is a most liberating thing you can do each day. When you come back, you can take a few more deep breaths and slowly open your eyes. Invariably you'll feel a sense of wellbeing and even bliss. You've just downloaded your real self and you are now full of vigour as you move back into the day again. You can move back to the world of "doing" from that of "being".

It's like a mini-being-break with Alexander.

The beauty about those little Green Platform 60-Second Time Out "being" moments is that you can do them while in the office, in the car and do them at various intervals throughout each day, every day while sitting, walking, waiting or queuing.

In fact, you can get a new slant on life with these Green Platform 60-Second Time Out moments. You know the way it is when you are in a long queue in a shop, or at an airport, or are part of a traffic jam.

Every week we encounter at least one or more of these irritating time-wasting problems in our life. Really, though, they are just moments to be transformed with a Green Platform 60-Second Time Out trip.

Now we can turn something we have always perceived as a negative and irritating problem into a positive interlude. You click into Green Platform 60-Second modes in these instances and instead of writing a story in your head that you're going to be late for the next thing you had planned to do, you can welcome the respite from "normal doing" to slip into a refreshing moment of "being".

You can go internal, get your mind to stop its reeling off thoughts together and come straight into the present moment where you are and meditate there in front of people without anyone realising it.

Once you get over the feeling that what you are doing is a little bit weird or eccentric, it becomes a wonderful aid in your day. By taking these little time-outs, you start to feel re-energised, connected and un-alone in life and suddenly your day becomes more enjoyable.

Driving our children Genevieve and Fionn down to the train for college in the morning means that we go through one set of traffic lights at McDonald's in Bray where more often than not, motorists are caught for a minute. It's one of the few moments in my day when I welcome 'Red' into my life. I am probably one of a small number of people who embrace being caught at that light because it gives me the opportunity to do a few little exercises that get me on the Green Platform.

If I get my minute outside McDonald's, I click into another realm, a higher one of enjoyment so that by the time I reach the train station two minutes down the road, I am a different person.

However if Genevieve or Fionn are engaged in an animated conversation about the joys of another day at college, then the Green Platform 60-Second Time-Out is put on hold until the way back.

If I don't manage to catch that traffic light on the way down, I am almost guaranteed to get one on the way back to kick-start my day with one of those 60-Second encounters with myself.

It would be untrue to say that one of those moments will sustain you for a day or a week. It won't. I do them maybe twice, or three times or five times or 10 times or whatever the particular day allows me. Most days we all have so many opportunities to use one of those Green Platform 60-Second 'packages' but don't realise it.

Now that you are aware of that fact, what's stopping you? You can start it first thing in the morning by sitting upright on the side of your bed and getting into the groove by switching off everything except your mental stroll into the present. If you can't do it there, well the chances are you either take public transport or drive into work. Just check out next time the number of opportunities that arise in your pre-work day for you to undertake one or more Green Platform 60-Second Time-Outs.

On the other hand, if you are staying at home working in the house, then once the other people are out the door and out of your way, you can make a habit of choosing a room ... the kitchen at the table, or the living room on an upright chair ... the bathroom or bedroom to click into this 60-second encounter. It works. If you can turn that Green Platform 60-Second moment into a two or three minute respite from your "doing" day, so much the better.

If you can do two or three of those moments each day, you will be surprised at the amount of real refreshment you find injected into your life. It is a true source of energy. And one that brings an awareness to you that life is simple yet joyful. With this perspective, life is so much more fun and so much easier to negotiate on a day-to-day basis. As we saw already, we never lose our inner joy. It's always there. We just lose our connection with it. If you cut the electric wire to your reading lamp, you'll never get light. All you need to do is reconnect the wires, turn on the switch and then you have light.

Can you automatically ask yourself key questions like: "What story and energy am I bringing to my own day and to those I encounter? From which platform? Am I giving positive energy and joy from deep inside or am I sapping energy with the mental noise in my head on the Red Platform?"

A Buddhist monk was marching for justice one time in Bangkok. There were batons flying and tear gas spraying all over the place. A reporter asked him: "How are you remaining so calm in the midst of this chaos?"

"I never leave my place of meditation and inner peace," he replied with a smile.

The great challenge in life is to be aligned with the present moment, with life as it is. If I get the wrong change in a shop, acceptance does not mean that I don't bring it to the attention of the shopkeeper. No, I say: "I'm sorry but there is a mistake in my change."

Acceptance and then PAN – Positive Action Now. No ranting. No raving. No anger. No verbal attack on the person. This is sometimes very difficult for people to grasp. In workshops and courses there is often a huge resistance to 'acceptance' because people equate acceptance with apathy, indifference or a meek acquiescence of things as they are. People think: "If I bring acceptance to this, nothing will change." Actually nothing could be further from the truth.

Resentment and resistance to the present situation will do more to hamper real change than anything else. There is a much better chance of positive change when I accept the 'is-ness' of a situation. What we resist will persist and we create what we defend against.

Where attention goes, energy flows. We should be putting attention on what we want, not on what we don't want. Yet we are almost culturally programmed to focus on what we don't want. "If I bring acceptance to the situation, then nothing will change?" The change that's based on an embraced acceptance of reality is a powerful platform for positive action and real lasting change.

The real myth is that we have to feel bad for something to change. Negative emotions block our ability to act wisely and they also block our mental ability to determine right action. Never make a major decision when you are feeling bad or you'll make a bad decision.

Actions we take when we are angry or frustrated tend to be reactions and not well thought through. We are instinctively reacting out of pain rather than taking inspired action in a meaningful way.

The more I try not to think about something, or stop something or fight against something, the more of it I bring into my life.

Mother Teresa was asked once would she join a march against war. She said: "No, but when you have a march for peace, I'll be there."

We've had a war on drugs, the fight against poverty and we've been tackling crime for years but they are all still there. Instead of anti-poverty campaigns we should be talking of wealth creation campaigns encouraging entrepreneurs to create jobs.

Fr Sean Connaughton worked as a Columban missionary in the Philippines for many years. He saw a lot of poverty, hunger and unemployment. He didn't spend too much time whinging and whining about the problems. He accepted the situation and activated PAN: "Positive Action Now."

He went to Bangladesh and learned all about micro-finance and the Grameen Bank from Dr Muhammad Yunus. He came back to the Philippines and set up the Grameen Bank. Through it small groups of people, mainly women, were able to get seed finance to set up their businesses. They were trained to be responsible for their businesses and for each other.

When Sean left the Philippines in 2007 he left 17,000 entrepreneurs running their own businesses and creating employment. When he returned as a guest to the Grameen Bank Annual Conference in 2010 there were 30,000 entrepreneurs running their own business and creating massive employment.

He truly set up a wealth creation campaign that is self-sustaining, self-nourishing and self-propagating. Instead of going into victim-mode, he focused on solutions and took positive action on the Green Platform. In the process he took thousands of people off the Red Platform of poverty, injustice and oppression and on to the Green Platform of justice, peace and sustainable wealth with him.

There is a difference between moving from what we don't want and moving towards what we do want. I like to imagine that each one of us has an invisible cup inside of us. Then we all have a little spoon like a dipper. In every encounter with another person, every meeting no matter how casual, I use my spoon to put a few drops into your cup.

I either put in a few drops that are positive, uplifting and constructive and make you feel happier instantly on the Green Platform, or else I say mean, hurtful things and drain your energy on the Red Platform.

With the poison drops I am your average Red Platform energy vampire. But when I put in some positive drops that are genuine and sincere I accelerate and expand your energy and your happiness on the Green Platform.

The only thing that is missing in a situation is what I'm not bringing to it while I'm on the Red Platform – the joy that is the springboard of positive action on the Green Platform. There is the need to accept the situation as if I had chosen it and that is always the challenge. For the person who loses his job or whatever else strikes us down in our lives, the accepting, allowing and embracing of the present moment is the same.

To start this process on the Green Platform I must be the change I want to see in the world as Gandhi once said. I must realise how beneficial being this change on the Green Platform is to me and to all those I encounter.

I am very surprised by the number of people who continue to come up to me and say the concept of the Green Platform changed their lives. I tell them I know exactly what they mean because it changed my life as well.

Once you understand that joy is something you want in your life as much as possible every day you will move onto a different plain. Life is much more than one darn thing after another.

When someone said to Mother Teresa that she was doing extraordinary things, she replied: "No, we are not doing extraordinary things here. We are doing very ordinary things with extraordinary love and joy."

Would you ever find a better description of life on the Green Platform?

When the man said to her: "I wouldn't do what you are doing here, not even for a million dollars."

She replied: "Neither would I."

She certainly captured the balance between "being" and "doing". She knew fully who she was "being", during all her "doing". Everyone who came in contact with her benefited.

When you get your "doing" and your "being" in balance, you tend to have a strong positive Self-Image.

The strongest force in the human personality is the need to remain consistent with how we define ourselves, our Self-Image, and that's what we'll look at next – the power of your Self-Image to determine which platform your live on, Green or Red.

CHAPTER 13

How Self-Image Defines Or Confines You

YOUR Self-Image is the inner picture you have of yourself. It's the way you see yourself in your imagination. The strongest force in the human personality is the need to remain consistent with how we define ourselves, how we see ourselves – our Self-Image.

The you you see is the you you'll be.

Most of us are not even aware that we have a Self-Image. It's a powerful internal thermostat inside each of us that the subconscious uses to self-correct up or down to our perceived image of ourselves. We cannot rise above our Self-Image, and if we do, we will quietly and subtly sabotage ourselves and self-correct back down again.

If we drop below it, we will self-correct back up again to where you think you belong, to be the you that you see inside. Your thermostat at home controls the heat in the house just like our Self-Image controls your potential.

On the Green Platform we have a strong positive Self-Image that we self-correct up to as we gradually become the kind of person we dream of becoming – being the best that we can be.

On the Red Platform we have a low Self-Image where we consistently self-correct down to the worthless kind of person we believe we are. And even at that we are always hoping we won't be "found out."

As American psycho-cybernetics pioneer, Dr. Maxwell Maltz succinctly put it: "Self-Image sets the boundaries of individual accomplishment."

The Self-Image you have of yourself controls virtually all of your behaviours on a day-to-day basis. Very rarely will you do something that is not in line with that inner mental image that you have of yourself. The way you set goals, choose your values or react to life is never determined by who or what you are, but by who and what you think you are.

YOUR SELF-IMAGE

If you were asked to go into a room full of strangers and go up to every single one of them and introduce yourself with a smile on your face, would you do it? The reality is, unless you 'thought of yourself' as a naturally outgoing and likeable person, you probably wouldn't. The thought of it might even make you nervous. You might say something like: "Oh, that's not who I am." Or: "I'm not that kind of person."

How do you know who you really are? If you believe yourself to be shy, it is very unlikely that you will spark up conversations with strangers, even if you feel desperately lonely. If you believe that you have no willpower over ice-cream, it is unlikely that you will not eat it when it is around, even if you hate being overweight.

All permanent change is guided by a change in Self-Image. Temporary habits and emotional changes can be made without changing the core Self-Image. But these cannot last. If you believe that you are not someone who would go for a walk or a jog or a swim, you will not go even though you make many mental resolutions to get fit. Your inner champion, your Self-Image will win all the time.

"I am not a runner, swimmer or whatever." The "that's not me" takes over. "Get back to where you belong" is the inner scream from your Self-Image.

Your Self-Image is with you all day every day for better or worse. Generally for worse. We will ditch any level of success that does not match what it demands. A negative Self-Image says: "That's just me. It's the way I am. Take me or leave me. And if you really knew me, you'll leave me pretty fast."

A positive Self-Image: "I can be a new and better me. I can choose who I am. I can choose who I will be. The me I see is the me I'll be!"

Your Self-Image comes from two main sources: Firstly, from the people around you. Think about the two most influential people in your life and you will find that you have accepted at least some of their beliefs, whether they are useful or not. Normally people mention a parent or a teacher. Think of your five best friends. Generally, you will be the average of what they are. You'll level out at their average.

Secondly, the experiences that you've had growing up. When you reflect on your life, what are the certain key experiences that have made you the person you are today? Remember, our Self-Images are not so much the result of our experiences as they are the meaning that we give to those experiences. Our interpretations of those experiences. As we've seen already, the reality is that facts have no meaning. A situation has no meaning. Nothing has any meaning but the meaning we give it.

The mental image you hold of yourself controls what you perceive in the world because your Reticular Activating System (RAS) or Gatekeeper filters out information that isn't useful to you and brings in information that you see as useful or important.

WHAT IS YOUR GATEKEEPER RAS?

Your Gatekeeper RAS is a small network of neurons at the back of your brain but it acts as that filter (from the Latin word "retica" which means net.) It takes in and then sorts all the stimuli coming at you from your surroundings and places them either into the "important bin" or the "rubbish bin".

This Gatekeeper RAS area is about the size of one section of an orange or a small thumb. It acts like a spam filter on a computer.

It determines what you will notice and what you will not pay attention to. It acts like a sentry or guard or Gatekeeper at the door of your mind.

Your mind is literally creating your reality, the choices that you will consider and the solutions that you recognise. Your Gatekeeper RAS will let in anything that matches your current Self-Image, that's why it is so important to have a positive Self-Image on the Green Platform. If you have a negative Self-Image on the Red Platform it will be equally active in hoovering in all the bits and pieces of information from your environment to support and reinforce your negative low Self-Image.

The main functions of the Self-Image is to meet your emotional needs or secondary gain. If I'm overweight, I will contrive to keep myself overweight so that I don't have to get into any romantic situations. That's my secondary gain, the pay-off.

Secondly, it allows you to make rapid decisions.

"Will you sing?"

"No way, I'm not a singer."

You ask children in kindergarten: "Who here can sing?" And all the hands go up. "Me, me, me!"

Ask the same class when they are 12 years old and no hands go up. They will name a famous pop star. "She's a singer, but not me."

Your Self-Image also gives you consistency and credibility. Change can be very challenging. People would prefer a hell they know than a heaven they don't. They want to change but then they think: "But how would I handle all the attention?"

Familiarity is one of the deepest human needs. That's why people will leave one abusive partner and then link up with another abusive partner. Familiarity.

Most people just accept the Self-Image they were 'given' instead of designing and installing the one they truly want. Even though you can't fight against your Self-Image, you can change it. You can design and install a new Self-Image.

How do you design and install a new Self-Image that will be the one you really want? If you change your Self-Image to think of yourself as you want to be, then you will automatically self-correct up and become that new person.

The key to changing your Self-Image from a negative miserable "poor me" one on the Red Platform to a powerful positive one on the Green Platform is understanding this fact: our subconscious mind cannot distinguish a real experience from an imagined one.

If I vividly imagine something, and feel deeply what it's like to achieve that something, to be that someone, then that becomes real for the subconscious and is ripe for manifestation into my life.

Of course this new Self-Image on the Green Platform has to be realistic and stretching for you. There's no point in visualising yourself as a famous pianist if you are tone deaf, have no fingers and don't play an instrument.

Think of change as something that happens from the inside out. As you believe yourself to be this new person on the Green Platform, your behaviour will naturally follow. This is the secret to creating long-term change. The good news is that changing your Self-Image isn't difficult when you follow some key steps.

The first step is visualisation. Spend some time designing, dreaming, imagining the person who you want to be. How you'd like to think, act and feel about things and yourself. Feel this feeling deeply. Assume the feeling of your new Self-Image as if it is fulfilled.

Once you have a clear, inspiring idea of who you want to be, install it. Make it real by thinking of specific situations and see, hear, and feel yourself acting as if you are this new person. The more you do this the more you train yourself to act this way and become this new person, naturally. You act as if you are that kind of person until you actually become that kind of person. You don't just fake it until you make it, you fake it until you actually become it.

That's the first step. Visualisation.

The you you SEE is the you you'll be. Anyway, how can you be it unless you first see it. Once you see it, and believe it, then you'll be it, you'll become it on the Green Platform.

The second step is Green Platform PowerTalk or affirmations or auto-suggestions or incantations. By that I mean you need to have a positive present-tense statement of your realistic but stretching goal or new Self-Image as if it is already there, accomplished, completed. First you visualise it, you see it in your mind's eye, and then you affirm that this new person is really you."

"I am confident, positive, strong and secure."

"I am always radiating positive energy."

"I am confident of achieving all my written goals."

"Every day in every way I am getting better and better."

"I am ..." is the start of all self-image change beliefs. No one did the "I am" bit better than Muhammad Ali or Cassius Clay as he was known when he started making headlines.

"I am the greatest," he said and while some saw this as arrogant, for Ali it was vital at a time when he was being thrown out of restaurants and drapery shops that he affirmed inside that he was somebody great. His grandmother told him to say these words over and over, and someday she said maybe he'd believe them and others would believe them. Although he probably never even heard of the Green Platform, with his: "I am the greatest," he was stepping on to it.

The rest is history.

You can use those two great words "I am" to launch yourself with a new positive Self-Image on the Green Platform or to bury yourself with a negative Self-Image on the Red Platform. You choose.

"I am confident, positive, strong and fit," or "I am doubtful, negative, weak and flabby."

"I am now enjoying this session in the pool," or "I am someone who hates swimming."

So when you want to change an action habit, when you want to feel more adventurous, when you want to finish all the things you start, then your Self-Image must transform from what it is now into what you want it to be. Switch the slides in your head. See the new you. Feel the feeling of being the new you. When you see yourself not as you are but as you can become, you stimulate incredible growth and incredible change. It really is a case of where attention goes, energy flows. Again, on the Green Platform we always put our attention on what we want, not on what we don't want. We put attention on the Self-Image we want.

When we put attention and focus on what we don't want we magnetically attract more of what we don't want. What we resist will persist on the Red Platform. When we put attention, focus and energy on what we want, the kind of person we want to be on the Green Platform, then we get more of what we want and become more like that person.

A good coach or parent will say: "I see you as ..." and then the team member or child will self-correct up to the newly implanted Self-Image. At the age of four children have a strong Self-Image and high self-esteem. By the age of 14, 98 per cent of children have a negative one. By the time they are 18 years old, 96 per cent have a negative Self-Image.

That's because on average we parents speak to or rebuke our children negatively 90 per cent of the time. "People will not remember what you said, and they may not remember what you did, but they will always remember how you made them feel," as Maya Angelou famously said.

By the time a child is 12 years old, they've received 100,000 Negative Belittling Remarks (NBRs) or put-downs. So how does a parent correct a child when they do something wrong in a way that doesn't dent and smash or damage their Self-Image?

First, there's the traditional Red Platform way that crushes their Self-Image: "You are a bold boy. You are a naughty girl. You're very bold. You're very naughty!"

Then there's the Green Platform way where you separate the person from the problem, the doer from the deed, the performer from the performance – or in theological language, the sinner from the sin:

"That was a bold thing to do. You're too good for that. Next time..." Then you create a picture of excellence for next time.

It's Green Platform NTT, Green Platform "Next Time Thinking."

In this way, you can be very tough on the problem, and very gentle on the person. Imagine that everyone's Self-Image is like a balloon, and you are carrying that balloon on needles taped to your fingers. You carry it very carefully or you'll burst it. That's how careful we have to be with someone's Self-Image.

Children would benefit enormously and their Self-Image on the Green Platform would zoom up to a new level if they received more Positive Affirming Remarks (PARs). PARs on the Green Platform are where you affirm someone in their gifts in a way that is genuine and sincere by consistently catching them doing things right.

The need to remain consistent with our Self-Image is at the core of our being. To be "like ourselves," to be "where we belong" in our comfort zone, is more important than being hugely wealthy, or successful or even more important than winning a game.

Eighty per cent of the people who won multiple millions in the Lottery in the US took just five years to spend it, get rid of it and get back in debt. Being "like themselves," was much more important than being hugely wealthy.

The mediocre Self-Image on the Red Platform or comfort zone is the greatest enemy of the human potential. A man told me some time ago that he was down playing golf in Wexford.

"I was playing fantastic. Unbelievable. Tiger (Woods) or Rory (McIlroy) or Pádraig (Harrington) wouldn't play as good for the first nine holes. But I kept telling my golfing friends: 'I don't normally play like this. This isn't me at all.' Then all the alarm clocks went off in my head."

So what did he do for the second nine holes?

Yes, self-corrected back to where he thought he belonged. Back to his negative self-image on the Red Platform. Then he had that perverse pleasure of being right.

"See, I told you I was useless. This is the real me at golf."

That's why the single biggest challenge with sports teams or players or anyone going for daily exercise is to get them to see themselves as champions or excellent performers in a manner that is realistic and stretching ... to discover their new Self-Image and self-correct up to that.

Muhammad Ali's mission now is to help every man, woman and child to be the greatest they can be. He wants to pass on his grandmother's wisdom about the power of a positive Self-Image that radically changed his life and the lives of millions of poor people around the world who benefit from his Ali Fund. A new positive Self-Image on the Green Platform is all about excellence, but without any trace of arrogance. For better or worse, "the you you see, is the you you'll be."

And of course, none of this works unless you do.

CHAPTER 14

It's So Easy To Miss 'The Gorge'

WHEN we're tearing along headlong for a destination, caught up in destination addiction and missing every step of the journey, we are unconsciously living on the Red Platform. Life is all about getting there and postponing life until some later time.

When we are fully alive, present and enjoying every step of the journey we are consciously living on the Green Platform. I learned this lesson one day in Japan, and later on in Taiwan.

The Japanese call a moment of enlightenment a "satori."

I remember once visiting Japan when I was working as a Columban missionary priest in Asia. While I was there a friend brought me to visit a Buddhist monastery. In the spirit of dialogue I asked a monk there what Zen Buddhism was all about.

He smiled and said: "It would take you 40 years to learn Zen Buddhism."

"But I don't have 40 years at the moment," I laughed. "Can you give it to me in one sentence?"

"Yes, I can, but it will take you 40 years to live it."

"Okay, give it to me."

"You are only doing what you are doing. Understand that the point of power is in the present moment. Presence is all that matters. Now, the present moment doesn't happen fast, it happens deep. Dive in."

He totally understood the "being" and "doing" balance. "Who are you being when you are changing your child's nappies or diapers? Who are you being when you are driving to work? Who are you being when you are milking the cows?"

You are a human being, not a human doing. You are a spiritual being having a human experience, not a human being having the odd spiritual experience. My eyes were opened one day many years ago when together with a few friends, we decided to walk the famous Taroko Gorge in Taiwan.

That day I had my "satori."

At the time I was working as a priest in Taiwan and every now and again a group of us would go to see some well-known place in that part of the world.

Three of us had decided to walk the gorge. It takes about five and a half hours to go from end to end of this wonderful phenomenon. With one Irish friend and one from New Zealand, we decided we would clip a fair chunk off the normal walking time by setting out at a fast pace.

With arms swinging and legs churning, the three of us charged out of the blocks and must have looked like army men in civilian clothes as we marched to our destination.

As we got into our stride and were really warming to the task at hand a few hours into our trek, we noticed near the end of one long straight stretch that there was a group of Chinese Buddhist nuns up ahead sitting serenely near – of all things – a Hi-Ace van.

It seemed out of place and even amusing to have such a mode of transport for these eight Sinead O'Connor lookalikes with their shaven heads and simple grey clothing.

As we drew nearer to where they were located, I was forced to slow down to tie the lace that had worked itself loose on my right runner. The other two lads kept going – we all had a clock running in our heads and didn't want to slow down – and as I stood upright again, my thoughts were to get back into the peloton before the two leaders totally burned me off.

Just as I was making headway in the chase to catch up, one of the nuns waved at me and said: "Just a moment, please."

Reluctantly I stopped and headed over to where she was stationed. My head was telling me I would miss the gorge if I lost too much time on my two colleagues but at the same time, I couldn't ignore her by just waving and walking on.

As I crossed to where she was, things raced through my mind. "Maybe they have a problem with the van and need me to try to start it or fix a puncture that they have picked up on their way to this remote place."

When I arrived where they were, she didn't smile or offer a hand to shake but looked quizzically at me.

"Excuse me," she began gently but firmly, "but do you realise you're missing the gorge."

I was slightly perplexed at the remark.

"What? Missing the gorge? How do you mean, I'm missing the gorge?" I asked.

She pointed back down to where we had come from and said in very clear simple Chinese: "From the moment I saw you coming along in the distance, I knew you three people had to be from the West. That's why I am telling you that you're missing the gorge."

"Missing the gorge?" I repeated, not really comprehending what she was on about.

Seeing that I wasn't getting it, she pointed to a spot and said: "Sit down, please."

I did what she asked more in bemusement than anything else.

That invitation was followed up with another.

"Close your eyes," she said, emphasising the three words independently as if I was a little boy in school.

I closed my eyes.

As I did, she said in the most gentle of tones, "Now just listen."

At that moment, I had a mental image of the two friends looking back at me and laughing at the fun of it as I sat with my eyes closed. Then I decided to forget about them and myself and do what the nun had asked.

I just listened.

At first I heard nothing or at least I could discern very little. Then slowly as if someone had opened up a window, a myriad of sounds slowly began tapping my consciousness.

Not unexpectedly, the first sound to make an imprint was the force of the water spraying over the rocks at the bottom of the gorge. It wasn't just the waterfall that I heard but the reverberating echo that came back up from the rocks below right along the gorge.

This sound came on the breeze that I could almost feel wafting gently through the trees and the bushes growing around and at the sides of the gorge.

Almost magically behind this little symphony of sound that was playing in the gorge, I heard a soloist – a birdsong that drifted operatic-like across the area like a soothing balm.

My friend the nun obviously judged that by now my senses had begun to take in the music of the gorge. She whispered: "Open your eyes now, and this time look and see, really see."

I opened my eyes as she had directed.

Immediately I felt more clued in. Now I could see the blueness of the water plunging to extinction in the foam below. Then the white froth of its resurrection surfing on the deeper dark colour at the bottom.

These vivid pictures contrasted with the strength of the grey-black rocks, the green-dressed trees and the frolicking wild plants jutting out of the crevices.

In more remote areas, the flowers were blooming in a patchwork quilt of colours. Violets and pinks. Oranges, reds and yellows. An iridescence completed by the duck-egg blue sky, acting like a dome above this theatre of senses.

"Now, three times I want you to breathe in deep, the gorge," the nun whispered.

I obeyed.

One.

In... out.

Two, in... out.

Three, in... out... the gorge."

I filled my lungs with air. Nature's crisp, fresh air.

Not polluted stuff like you had to breathe every day around Taipei at that time.

I was now totally relaxed and for the first time, looked earnestly at my mystical new friend.

Her countenance had changed totally and as she turned her little porcelain chin up to me, she said mischievously: "See, you were missing the gorge?'

I smiled warmly, bowed to her and told her that I agreed I was missing the gorge until I met her.

I looked up towards the horizon to see how far the others had gone. They were quite some way up the gorge from me by this stage.

She could read my thoughts.

Her mood had changed again, this time to one of chiding.

"I hope the way you are rushing around is not symbolic of the way you live your life," she said.

I didn't answer but waved and bowed as I began to walk on.

I knew of course that she was right. It was a symbol of my life.

Like many of us today I was caught up in destination addiction.

Getting there.

Missing the journey.

Missing the gorge.

We don't need new landscapes. We need new eyes to see the landscapes that are already there. "If I change the way I look at things, then the things I look at change." She got me to do that.

Once she changed the way I looked at the gorge, heard the gorge, breathed in the gorge ... the gorge changed.

If I change the story in my head the reality I look at changes. We don't see things as they are, but rather as we are.

In a word, she got me off the busy, problem cluttered rushing, dashing, hurrying mental noise on Red Platform and on to the peace and tranquillity of the Green Platform.

Insights and breakthroughs come from a tranquil silent place inside. Awareness meets new insights in silence. Our minds are like a lake. If the waves are tossing 30 feet high in a storm, even if you throw in the Eiffel Tower, the lake would not notice it. But if the lake is flat like glass, then the lake will notice the ripples of the tiniest pebble landing on the water. As the poet WH Davies said: "What is this life if full of care, we have no time to stand and stare."

This mystical Buddhist nun saw me on the Red Platform, full of care, with no time to stand and stare and she gently switched me on to the Green Platform of peace, joy and harmony.

When we look at people what do we see? Years ago if you were a traditional psychologist you were trained to see everything that was wrong with people. You were trained to be problem spotter. Not a light spotter. Not a magnificence spotter. Not a unique brilliance spotter.

The beauty of the gorge was already in me. This nun just brought it out of me.

I have been telling people this story ever since I had my experience with the nun and the Gorge. I've told it in seminars attended by hundreds of people, to clients in one to one courses or in small groups, to friends, and even to the odd stranger I've met at airports or sat besides on long transatlantic journeys. The famous customer care author Colin Shaw asked if could he use the story in his book, "Revolutionise Your Customer Care."

He saw the gorge as our customers and he feels that most of the time we miss not only who our customers really are but also what our customers really want. Often we're scratching where they're not itching. He called the first chapter, "Are You Missing The Gorge?"

The people who have heard it most often, of course, are my family. And sometimes, it's been used to teach me a lesson.

Like the time I was stressed out – up to 90 – trying to get Genevieve (when she was a child getting swimming lessons) out of the house on time for her class in Dublin. We had 10 minutes to make the six miles journey in traffic and I was fairly stressed, or as Victor Frankl would say, I was busy manufacturing my own stress.

Every parent and kid has heard a hundred versions of the stress scenario I was creating that day.

"Look at those trees, Daddy," Genevieve said, out of the blue, throwing me a ball from left field.

"Aren't they a lovely shade of green? They are my gorge. Are you missing your gorge today, Daddy?"

Game, set and match to Genevieve.

All I could do was laugh and say: "Thanks for that, Genevieve, you are absolutely right." That little reprimand helped me in no small measure down the years and more recently in my dealings with Alexander.

Because of his Mowat Wilson syndrome, Alex is among other things, doubly incontinent. I used to dread those three to five minutes when I would change his nappies (or diapers). They were moments I didn't look forward to. Nor did Alexander. Often he would cry and resist the nappy change.

Genevieve made me realise that "The Gorge" wasn't a Zen creation that was geographically placed in some magical oriental country thousands of miles away from Ireland.

It was on the road from Bray to Dublin on a swimming lesson day and it was in the house with Alexander any time he needed his nappy or diaper changed.

Genevieve's lesson to me was that it was no use telling some "Gorge Story" if I didn't live every second of its meaning.

Now I look forward to the nappy-changing times with Alexander. More than that I tell him we are going to have him all cleaned up in a jiffy and we are going to laugh and have fun while we are doing it. Alexander didn't change, but I did. Once I decided to bring joy from deep inside me to the changing-his nappy-challenge, he in turn picked up the positive vibrations and he changed.

Now he laughs and thinks it's great fun. We both changed from the 'Missing the Gorge' on the Red Platform to the 'being fully present, here, now' on the Green Platform.

Because I now laugh and have a happy face, he responds and shrieks with delight as I talk and sing and laugh and whistle while we are cleaning him up and making him smell of roses.

Alexander and I have made our own Gorge time – and we really enjoy it. The story of the Gorge is really the story of power in the present moment. You are only doing what you are doing. Don't miss the 'now.' Dive in as deep as you can to the present moment, whatever the context and say a deep Green Platform 'yes' to the present moment, as you say a deep 'no' to the Red Platform rushing, fussing, blaming and complaining.

When we are awake and aware we can be fully alive and aligned with life as it is or when we're unaware and sleepwalking through life we can feel and act and react in a non-aligned way.

We are either one with life, or two with life, raging against life with our never-ending list of 'shudas' or 'couldas'.

"You should have (shuda) been here yesterday."

"I could have (coulda) got better marks if only I had done some homework."

How many times in your life do you find yourself talking to someone only to discover that they are 'out to lunch.' Not present?

This kind of physically present but mentally absent thing is happening more and more. People are preoccupied with their thoughts, with their fears and their worries. They are, at best, only half with the 'now' in their lives.

This is such an important part of our living time to get right. If we get this 'now' understanding working correctly, most other things fall into place.

My wife Annette is from Bundaberg in Queensland, Australia. Her friend Fay told us a lovely story one time when we were visiting about the wonderful gift she and several of her friends received from a great Australian woman they all revered as a living saint.

That lady had the gift of healing others in her lifetime but she gave more than that. There were many times she helped people through severe traumas with her wisdom and understanding.

In her own life, she was diagnosed with cancer but never once allowed that to come between her and the good work she did automatically on a daily basis.

Nevertheless, she knew her time was short and as she became weaker, she called Fay and a number of her friends to her bedside one evening.

In the room they each found a gift from her in the most amazing, beautiful Japanese-styling wrapping. The women asked if they could open their presents to see what was inside.

However, her response to their requests took them all aback.

"My present to you is nothing more than 'the present' itself – it is a reminder to each one of you that every time you look at the present with its wrapping, you come back in to the present moment.

There is no present, no gift inside the box, inside the wrapping. Put it some place where you will see it several times a day, in your office or your kitchen or your workshop and use this present as a way of coming into the present moment – the now. Be fully present, here, now. If you do, it will be the best present I can ever give you."

What a wonderful legacy to leave to her friends... and one many of them still use to this day.

From a previous chapter we know that the Ego is hell-bent on keeping us away from that pathway. The Ego knows that once we enter through it into 'the now,' then his job as the false self disappears. He can worry us with guilt or regret about the problems of the past or the fears of the future but if we look at the "now" in our life, he is forced to get off our stage.

As you are reading this now, I want you to stop for a second and do the following. Forget everything except this exact moment. The present. The now.

Take a gentle breath and say to yourself: "Right now, I have nothing to be fearful of. In fact for this moment I am going to choose to be happy."

We are conditioned to allow ourselves to be ruled by an Ego who keeps our thoughts in the dark areas of fear from our past or our anxiety fuelled imagined future.

What a crazy place to live. When you think about it, there is only one place to live – and that is in the present moment.

Life is not measured by the number of breaths you take, but by the moments like that one in the gorge that take you breath away.

Your 'satori,' or times of enlightenment moments.

I had such a moment in 'The Gorge' but you don't need to go off thousands of miles to feel that 'satori'.

You can feel it right here and now by making that decision yourself to be happy... for now.

And that's what your life is... a series of present moments joined up.

Consider the following questionnaire that the British psychologist and author Robert Holden once asked a group of cancer patients to complete for him.

Robert is considered one of the world's foremost expert on happiness and is the founder of the 'Happiness Project.'

His simple question was: "Is cancer a gift, yes or no?"

Out of 325 people, 303 or 93 per cent answered 'yes.'

Afterwards Robert told them he didn't personally believe any illness was a gift. But he marvelled at those who had the intelligence and courage to turn such a heavy burden as cancer into one.

It was his way of reminding us that we can make our lives full of gifts if, as the old Roger Miller song says: "We can be happy if we have a mind to."

From now on, you and I can turn situations around by asking ourselves: "What is the gift in this? Where is the seed of a greater benefit?"

So many times I've met people who've been devastated by a diagnosis of a severe illness. They see no gift in it. At that time they see no benefit in it.

Yet a few years later they told me that their illness was actually life-changing. They were able to see it as a most profound gift.

Just asking those two Green Platform power questions, "What's the gift?" or "What's the benefit" will help you to look for the advantage or opportunity in every moment even where you have to face adversity.

Of course, we have to look into the future, have a vision and plan, but then the key is to see the vision or the goal clearly and then detach from it. All our energy has then to go into the present moment. The "now".

THE GREEN PLATFORM FORMULA

1. Crystal-clear, high-definition, in-focus goal with a precise step-by-step plan.

2. Detach and release the goal like a balloon.

3. Now all your energy goes into the present moment's action as you implement your plan. Enjoy every step of the journey.

I know one young hurler who would not agree with this. He felt that having a clear vision of his team as champions was putting the cart before the horse, or tempting fate, or getting too big for his boots, or counting his chickens before they were hatched. All kinds of stuff like that.

But I explained to him that if I'm driving from Dublin to Galway or New York to San Francisco, I absolutely need to know where I'm going. I need to know my destination. Otherwise I'll end up in Killarney or San Diego.

But if on the way at Athlone and I'm up through the roof of the car trying to see Galway then I'll be over the ditch in no time. Then I'm attached to the outcome.

You must have a destination. Then detach and enjoy every step of the journey. Beware of destination addiction and missing the gorge. Now it's this game, this shot, this tackle, this work day, this classroom lecture, this family evening that really matters and these places are where you put all your energy.

Chuang Tzu (300 BC) explained the same idea with reference to the art of target shooting. "When an archer is shooting for nothing he has all his skill. If he shoots for a brass buckle he is already nervous. If he shoots for a prize of gold he goes blind or sees two targets – he is out of his mind.

"His skill has not changed. But the prize (the outcome) divides him. He cares now about winning. He thinks more of winning than of shooting and the need to win drains him of power."

His attachment to the outcome or the prize caused him to lose the present, the now, and the moment. Process is lost in outcome addiction. The future fear-fuelled focus destroys the now. Fear replaces freedom and fun. Then the action in the now withers and shrivels and loses its free-flowing power.

The journey is there to be enjoyed, not endured. Like the Greek poet Constantine Cavafy's famous journey to Ithaka:

"When you set out for Ithaka,
ask that your way may be long,
full of adventure and full of instruction.
Have Ithaka always in your mind.
Your arrival there is what you are destined for.
Better it last for years, so that when you reach the island you are
old and rich with all you have gained on the way and
not expecting Ithaka to give you wealth.
Rich with all you have gained on the way."

"Rich with all you have gained on the way."

Isn't that a marvellous line? Ithaka "gave you a splendid journey. Without her you would not have set out."

That's the purpose of a destination. The mountain of success is going to be very lonely if we do not enjoy the climb, the view, and the companionship on the way up. Terry Fox ran with an artificial leg 3,339 miles across Canada to raise money for cancer research. Twenty-four miles a day. How did he do it? One telegraph pole at a time. Just to the next telegraph pole. Unfortunately, mid-way through the cancer returned and claimed his life but what he achieved before that was remarkable. He broke it down to small segments. If we don't do that, it is easy to be overwhelmed.

Stu Mittleman, world record holder for Ultra-Distance Running said: "I never ran 1,000 miles. I could never have done that. I just ran one mile a thousand times."

When I was a young boy growing up I often heard this rhyme:

"Worry not over the future,
The present is all that thou hast.
The future will soon be the present,
And the present will soon be the past."

There is a lot of wisdom in those four simple lines. The past is history. The future is mystery. The precious present is all we have. It is the greatest gift you can give yourself. It's a gift that only you can give. You always have a choice. You can choose to be happy now in the present moment, or you can choose to be happy, "when ..." or "if ..." It's always your choice.

The Green Platform is about having a dream, a vision and clear goals but always living fully in the present, enjoying every step of the journey and fully experiencing the gorge. The mountain of success can easily turn into the barren Red Platform if we haven't been living on the Green Platform during the journey – enjoying the climb, the view and the fun with the friends who have made the journey with us.

As Edmund Hillary said: "It is not the mountain we conquer but ourselves." On the Green Platform we have a vision, clear goals and plans, but we live fully in the present moment, fully experiencing the gorge. Awake. Aware. Here. Now. How simple it is to see that we can only be happy now. And that there will never be a time in our lives when it is not 'now.'

On the Green Platform we are fully present, fully alive in the 'now', inspired by some great purpose, by some extraordinary life-transforming project. But how do we avoid destination addiction in our ordinary everyday activities? That is the question I will endeavour to answer in the next chapter.

CHAPTER 15

The Folly Of Destination Addiction

DESTINATION addiction is the preoccupation with the idea that happiness is somewhere else. Usually in the future. We are on a runaway train bound for a station called next.

Ultimately, destination addiction is life on the Red Platform. Everything will be better soon, and the life we dream of is in the future somewhere and we hope to catch up with it some time soon. Red Platform destination addiction says we have to rush through as many experiences as quickly as possible. These are the symptoms:

◆ Whatever I'm doing I'm thinking about what comes next, some more important event later today or tomorrow.

◆ I cannot afford to stop because I always have to be somewhere else. On the move. Busy. Rushing.

◆ I'm always in a hurry even when I don't need to be. It's a deeply ingrained habit. As I live on my busy, hectic, go-go Red Platform I don't let that car out in front of me because I might lose some time. (I've never ever not let a car out in traffic when I was in a hurry that I didn't feel worse afterwards. And I've never let a car out in front of me that I didn't feel better afterwards.)

◆ I'm always promising that next year will be less crazy, less busy, less hectic.

◆ I never commit fully to anything in case something better might come along.

◆ I hope my next big success will finally make me happy.

◆ I'm forever thinking that I should be further ahead than where I am now.

◆ On this unconscious insidious Red Platform, I'm consistently and persistently missing the gorge.

The enemy is destination addiction ... the living in the "not now." Do I eat a banana to get to the end of it or to enjoy every bite, or am I even aware that I'm eating it. Can I just enjoy the journey?

On the other hand part of the Latin root for "grace" is "Gratus" which means to welcome with gratitude.

Classical literature is full of great thinkers who thought that the key to a rich life is to welcome the here and now.

Despair is always five minutes ahead, never now. These great thinkers encourage us to "enjoy the precious present." Once you can enjoy the precious present, you are on the Green Platform.

Mystics, philosophers and quantum physicists all agree that the stuff of now is the stuff of the future. Have a clear goal, detach from it, and live fully and passionately in the now with all your heart and all your soul and all your might, and you'll hit the zone. The flow. Optimal experience. Grace is possible in every moment.

Therefore the simplest way to transform any task into a potential "flow experience" or "zone" is to set ourselves an intention, purpose or goal in relation to that task.

In cases where that task is mundane, repetitive, or simply not interesting to us, our intention need not be related to the actual task.

For instance, living the intention of 'being fully present' can turn a boring drive into a Zen meditation; living the intention of "performing with energy, enthusiasm and excitement and as if it's the most important thing in the world" can turn the washing of the dishes or changing a nappy or diaper into the most enjoyable activity.

Pat Henry, the Irish personal trainer to the stars gave a talk a number of years ago in Dublin.

Pat spent years in the east studying Zen and other Eastern arts. He can put his body into all kinds of states. But he won't let people in his gym watch television or listen to music when they're working out. He can see the auras. When one is working on a muscle with all of one's attention on that muscle, there is a totally different response than when the person is distracted with their attention somewhere else.

Where attention goes, energy flows.

It's like hitting a golf shot while listening to a world cup final penalty shootout. The golf shot's not going to be great. Pat told the meeting about one time when he was out just washing the car one morning, his wife asked him what he was at because he had this incredible look on his face. He said he was in Zen meditation. When he washes the car he washes the car. Period.

Fully in the present. No regrets about the past. No worries about the future. Just fully present on the Green Platform answering the two great mystical questions:

"Where am I?"

"Here."

"What time is it?"

"Now."

If we cannot discover Zen meditation washing the dishes there's no way we'll find it in a cave on a mountain in Nepal or Tibet.

That's why the 'grace' I need for something next Tuesday will only come to me next Tuesday. Not now. Now is the goal. Now is the inner wisdom that coaches me in every moment. Now is when you get the 'notion.'

"I got this notion the other day ..."

Go to the woods or the mountain or the sea or the island to discover the moments of "I had a notion..." This is your intuition. Your gut feeling. That's inner wisdom coming out.

Busy-ness is the enemy of the great transforming notion, the inspired action idea.

The Chinese word for busy-ness is 'knife' or 'killing' and 'heart.' When we're busy we kill what the heart wants to achieve. The heart wants to connect, to observe, to drink in and to be aware and awake on the Green Platform. But we're too busy. Maybe tomorrow?

"It is only with the heart that one sees rightly," said the little prince. "What is essential to the heart is invisible to the eye."

'Now' is our teacher. "Am I living well now? What is life teaching me now? What's the best use of my time right now?"

Wisdom is knowing how to maximise the enjoyment of each moment. Being fully present enables people to give of their best and also to be able to receive the best that is on offer. Every day is a gift for those who really believe that every day is a gift.

There's a story in the orient about a monk who had a little bird on his shoulder. The bird could foretell the future. Each morning the monk would ask the little bird: "Is today the day?" meaning is today the day that I am going to die.

The bird would always reply: "No, but live it as if it is."

When the late Steve Jobs, the founder of Apple, had his terminal illness confirmed he resolved to live each day as if it were his last. In the present day and age, it seems like we've got to do everything really fast? Fast food. Fast driving. Life in the fast lane. But why?

Are the best musicians the ones who play the fastest? Are the best actors the ones who say their lines the quickest? Are the wisest people I know the fastest thinkers? Do the best golfers swing their clubs faster than anyone else?

Do the best athletes force the pace from the front for the entire race? Are the best leaders the ones who have overnight success? Are the most successful people on the planet always in a hurry? Are we getting ahead of ourselves? That's a perfect formula for getting on The Red Platform.

I once saw a documentary about the Maasai tribe running across the plains of Africa. After about 25 miles they stopped. The television reporter asked them why they had stopped. "We're waiting for our souls to catch up with us," they said.

They needed to reconnect and get back on The Green Platform.

The Now is the Portal to the Zone

The now is the portal to the zone that footballers sometimes talk about. Runners sometimes call it the flow. Musicians talk about being in the groove.

It's when everything flows and appears easy. It's like things are happening in slow motion. You have total confidence and self-belief. You are at the top of your game. It's pure Green Platform.

Larry Bird of the Boston Celtics basketball team spoke one time of being in the zone and falling down near the basket and from virtually the ground trying a shot from a ridiculous angle because he was in the zone ... and it went in. He nailed it.

According to Mihaly Csikszentmihalyi (mee-hi chikk-sent-me-hi) from the university of Chicago, who spent over 30 years studying optimal experiences or flow, the one trait that constantly comes up in the research into creativity or flow or the zone is that these are most likely to occur when we are focused on only one thing at a time.

To get into the zone on the Green Platform it is critical to have a clear goal and then to detach from the goal or outcome. Flow is more likely to happen when an activity is intrinsically satisfying, when our attention is on the present moment performance now, rather than focused on the goal. When we do things not necessarily because it will make us look good, or make us money, but from the sheer love of doing the thing, we increase the likelihood in experiencing flow. Doing the thing itself has purpose and meaning.

This childhood natural experience is blocked when we become self-conscious around the age of five. We already begin to judge ourselves through the eyes of the people around us. We take our first faltering steps on the Red Platform. When we are able to become completely absorbed in a flow experience, we return to that pleasant state where what we are doing and experiencing becomes far more interesting than what other people might be thinking. We're back on the Green Platform.

Again, the secret of being happy on the Green Platform is not merely doing what one likes; it's liking what one does.

Happiness in not in things, it's in you. Joy flows to what you do from deep within you. And it's a platform that you can choose. It's Green not Red.

When Michaly Csikszentmihalyi completed his initial studies into "flow and the psychology of optimal experience" he was asked to summarise the findings in this 2,000-page document. After thinking for a moment, Csikszentmihalyi replied: "Every day the happy person does at least one challenging thing that stretches them."

Do it now and let the joy flow into every moment from deep within you. Once you do that, you are on the Green Platform. Your life will change for the better and the joy you get from day-to-day living will rise up to meet you. Once we're in 'flow' doing something, we are activating everything that is right and good about ourselves.

Oftentimes our history and culture in family life, education and business is focused more on what's wrong and bad about ourselves. This does enormous damage. One woman said to me recently: "I was reared in a Red Platform family."

Is there another way forward for families, for education and for business?

CHAPTER 16

The Truth About Myself

I HEARD a lovely Green Platform prayer recently that goes against the grain of everything I've ever heard before. It went: "Oh God, help me to realise the truth about myself today, no matter how beautiful it may be."

I grew up surrounded by negativity. It was part of our DNA, our history and our daily lives because we were presided over by a very negative God who forbade us from doing anything enjoyable. He was central to an over-riding negative religion which the Catholic Church championed for so many years up until recently, when thank God, common sense and some horrendous internal problems forced it to look at itself and change or die. Still, it came as quite a shock to me to consider the idea that we're basically good instead of being portrayed as rotten to the core.

The late great Irtish poet and philosopher John O'Donohue talked about this one time. He grew up near the Burren in Co. Clare with what he called a kind of Catholic rap.

"What is an occasion of sin?"

"Any person, place or thing that entices you to sin."

"Sin was everywhere," he said, "but somehow, divil the harm it did us."

The fact that we're good to the core should have been there all the time. Once we open up to the concept that we can see the good in ourselves, it stands to reason that it becomes much easier to see the good in others.

We've grown up in a very corrective world in business, in family and in education. Correct, correct, correct is the driving force. And correct often means criticising instead of encouraging.

In the 1930s, Carl Jung, the eminent thinker and psychologist put it this way: "Criticism has the power to do good when there is something that must be destroyed, dissolved or reduced, but it is capable only of harm when there is something to be built."

Imagine if we could look at people and see what's magnificent, noble, bright, brilliant and wonderful in them, and nurture and nourish all those lovely inner things, wouldn't it make such a difference?

Deep inside each one of us is a great and precious gift. It's our talent. It's our core genius. It's our blueprint for magnificence and all we have to do is become aware of it and download it. It's our gift to be used in the service of humanity. Everyone has a purpose in life, a unique gift or talent to give to others. When we blend this unique talent with service to others we experience the ecstasy and exultation of our own spirit. This indeed is the goal of all goals.

When Michelangelo was asked how he carved the beautiful statue of David in Florence, he replied, "I just saw David in the block of marble without blemish, and I just removed everything that wasn't David." That's the power of the uncared block and most of us are like that uncarved block of marble. There's a magnificent David inside of us all.

To know your gift you have to first see it and become aware of it. So look inside yourself and see that amazing inner David ... and release him.

Over 300 years ago, the Burmese army planned an attack to invade Thailand. At the time, the country was known as Siam. The Siamese monks were in possession of the most amazing Buddha statue. The statue is over 10 feet tall and weighs in excess of 2.5 tons. It is made of solid gold and is valued today at $200 million.

The monks were determined to protect the shrine that meant so much to them. While it was priceless to them for reasons that transcend money, they knew that the Burmese would stop at nothing to steal the statue because of its tremendous monetary value.

They covered the Golden Buddha with 12 inches of clay knowing that the warriors would totally ignore it and think it worthless. Sadly, the monks were slaughtered in the invasion and the secret of the Golden Buddha stayed hidden for two centuries. The Buddha itself though, remained safe.

In the mid-50s a monastery was to be relocated to make room for a new highway. The monks arranged for a crane to come and move the 'clay' Buddha to its new location. When the crane started to lift the statue, it was much heavier than expected and it began to crack. Wanting to protect the priceless shrine, the monks lowered it back down and decided to wait until the next day to bring in more powerful equipment.

To add insult to injury, the rains came so the monks lovingly covered the statue with tarps to keep the moisture away. In the dark of night, the head monk took his flashlight and went out to make sure the Buddha was adequately covered.

When the light of the flashlight shone into the crack of the clay, he saw a glimmer...a reflection of something underneath that shroud of clay. He started to carefully chisel away shards of clay to find that the glimmer grew brighter. Hours later, and all the clay removed...he was in the presence of a Buddha made of solid gold.

It now resides in The Temple of the Golden Buddha in Bangkok, Thailand. Every year, millions of people go there to see this magnificent work of art and to worship at his feet. And to think, it may never have been uncovered...

There is a magnificent David standing on a Green Platform inside of you. All you need to do is to polish up what is already there ... your inner blueprint for magnificence. It's only a matter of chipping away at the outer clay of limiting beliefs, fear and doubt ... and casting them out.

Thích Nhất Hạnh is a Vietnamese Zen Buddhist monk, teacher, author, poet and peace activist. He said one time: "People deal too much with the negative, what is wrong.... Why not try and see positive things, to just touch those things and make them bloom?"

By default we're conditioned to spot what's wrong with people, and catch them doing things wrong, rather than seeing all what's right with people and then catching them in the act of doing things right.

How many times when you were young or not so young have you heard the Red Platform question, "What's wrong with you?"

Where does your focus and attention go then? Straight to you subconscious with an unlimited excavation of all the things that are wrong with you and once you ask your subconscious a poison question like that it will get its JCB or Caterpillar Bulldozer and go to work. "You're looking for an occasion of sin? Well, here we go. Let's look."

Imagine the answer to that as your subconscious starts to discover all the things that you perceive are wrong with you?

Now your subconscious will have a field day excavating and digging up everything that's wrong with you. What will that do for your Self-Image? What will that do to help you discover your gift and enable you to use it in the service of humanity?

How many times have you heard the question: "What's right with you?" Yet there is so much right with you. Imagine all the lovely landscapes you could discover on that sacred quest. "What's an occasion of grace, of goodness, of kindness, of compassion, of unconditional love?" Now you're travelling in a different inner country. Different scenery. Different inspiration. Different answers.

Imagine your subconscious doing a kind of Google search inside discovering all the things that's right about you. How would that make you feel? On which platform would you land? What would that do for your Self-Image?

There's an enormous need to get on the Green Platform and shine a light on what is right. To catch people in the act of doing things well, right or just that little bit better. We learn to walk by learning how we walked, not by learning, recording, or filming and remembering how we fell. That would only help us to become great fallers.

Then as we continue to engage in a genuine way with people the need for continual praise goes down. The person-to-person engagement takes over. There's no need to turn children into little "praise-junkies."

Now it doesn't mean that there isn't badness and bad behaviour and people who do very bad things in the world. Of course there is. If all of humanity were just one person, we'd probably be certified "insane." We managed to land firmly on the Red Platform and killed one hundred million of our fellow human beings on this planet in just the last century. And we're still at it.

But change will only happen when we start to look for what's right in people and then bring it out of them, draw it out of them. That's education. Change can only happen when we switch platforms.

Start with your family because that's where everything begins and ends in our day. If you could see what's praiseworthy and wonderful in your spouse or children and then by communicating your feelings help to bring it out of them, just look at the sense of profound transformation you are starting to bring to the world by being on the Green Platform.

It all starts first and foremost with seeing yourself in a good light. Self-acceptance is the deepest and most profound thing that we can allow happen to ourselves.

Why?

Because it enables effortless change, self-improvement and happiness to flood into our lives. For this great deluge to sweep over us, it sometimes only needs the tiniest push. Like a twig stuck on a flowing river. Just a small nudge and it's off and flowing to new horizons.

I know from my own experience that there are many occasions when that is easier said than done. There are daily encounters and obstacles that not only make us doubt ourselves, but sap all our energy to fight back.

Albert Schweitzer, the great doctor who worked in Africa with the poorest of the poor, described it aptly when he remarked that: "Sometimes our light goes out."

When that happens, we land flat on our backs. The big question that sports people always claim is not the force of the knockdown but how you get back up on your feet. Sometimes you need an invisible helping hand to get going again.

Schweitzer believes the best way to rekindle was to be "blown to flame by an encounter with another human being. Each one of us owes enormous gratitude to those who have rekindled this inner light."

How right he was. A good friend is the best currency we can have in life. He or she will lift you up when you're down and just as importantly will keep you on an even-keel when you go astray.

Good friends help us to accept ourselves as we are because they will invariably point out our good points that we ourselves are inclined to denigrate. Explanations? Good friends don't need them and your enemies won't believe them. To good friends who understand you, no explanation is necessary. To those who don't understand you, no explanation is possible.

It is from this position of self-acceptance that we can move on to the next level of self-improvement. By studying, if we feel we want to re-educate ourselves in terms of a new career. Or to exercise more if, as many of us feel, we want to lose those pounds that have held us back physically for years.

I think though that we start off at the wrong place when we try to lose weight. I've seen people grab themselves by the midriff and publicly proclaim that they hate their bodies and can't be happy until they've lost all the weight.

They are putting the cart before the horse by postponing loving themselves until they are that different person and body sometime down the road in the future.

I prefer the Dawn French approach. We've all known and loved the English comedienne and actress for years and years as the one with the outsize figure who stars in The Vicar of Dibley and for her French and Saunders sketches.

Last year I read an interview with her where she revealed that she had lost an amazing seven and a half stone (105lbs). I thought the article would go on to highlight 'the new me' part of her life but instead I was astounded to read that she misses her old body. "I have a great fondness for that other body. I was never actually unhappy then so it is not the case that I was miserable then and am happy now."

She went on to bemoan the loss of the other Dawn's body by revealing that she could no longer swim all year round in the sea – something she loved to do. "Before, I had all this lovely blubber; I had my own wetsuit ... now I don't have enough flesh to keep me warm in the winter months."

"Lovely blubber." When would you hear any of us describe ourselves with such endearing remarks about being over-weight?

We reach for the negative self-belittling remarks and make ourselves unhappy in the process. Dawn did the opposite; she empowered herself. She was happy as an oversized woman and was happy as a new slim-line version of that same person.

What great self-awareness to have. She is an example that we can all follow in life and know it will be the best French lesson we can ever learn.

In fact there can be no self-improvement without self-acceptance. As Dawn showed, you should like yourself as you are. Then go on and enjoy the journey, as you become a new shape in the post-exercise and healthy-diet you have embarked on.

Don't postpone loving yourself until you hit the perfect weight because you are wasting precious days, weeks, months and maybe even years in your life. Dawn has shown us that losing weight is not the key to happiness but maybe that happiness could be one of the keys to losing weight.

You must accept yourself and love yourself, as you are first. Another woman said to me one time: "I get up at five every morning, I go for a half hour jog down by the river, I come back and I do 15 minutes Pilates, then I meditate for 20 minutes and I have a very healthy breakfast ... now why am I not happy?"

When I explained to her that self-acceptance comes before self-improvement, then she got it. She kept postponing happiness until she got to this ideal picture that she had in her mind.

As we learned from Dawn, if you don't love yourself when you are 180 pounds, there isn't a chance you'll love yourself when you are 150 pounds. Most of us live the second commandment backways. Love your neighbor instead of yourself. How about giving "as yourself" a try?

The Ego will try to hide at such times behind its three shadows of "then," "next," and "more," in his daily bid to make you feel unhappy. He wants you on the Red Platform. The Ego is quite literally that fearful thought within us that tells us happiness is not and never will be "now."

Your response to that must be that today is where you reside and the present moment is full of happiness. You are on the Green Platform. You are not prepared to wait until next week. Next June. Next year. Not until you get more time off, more pay, more holidays. But right this minute.

If you bring that single awareness to your life and become a Green Platform person, the Ego will disappear like a shadow in sunshine.

Self-awareness in our life should go hand in hand with how we deal with others. Just as it is important for you to have good friends, it is essential that we too are good friends to others.

But it is not quite as simple as it seems.

So much of our anger and frustration with others comes from wanting and expecting them to be something other than what they are.

Friends, colleagues and even acquaintances. We want to rewrite their stories and make them into what we think they should be. It's not acceptance, more of a conditional state of mind. Let me give you an example that shows the importance of kindness in our life.

In Ohio State University some years ago, one of the scientific research teams undertook a study in heart disease by feeding rabbits serious high-cholesterol diets to block their arteries. This was to duplicate and extrapolate what the effect on human arteries might be.

The research went very well. All the rabbits' arteries were blocked. The heart disease led to their deaths. Killed stone dead as they say.

There was a fly in the scientists' ointment though because one group of rabbits under examination bucked the trend. This group showed 60 per cent fewer symptoms. Which was baffling as nothing in these rabbits' physiology could account for their high-tolerance levels of the diet.

So what happened that made such a difference?

The discrepancy was a source of annoyance to the leaders of the group who set out to find why there was this clearly visible difference in their findings.

It took a while before they stumbled on the simple explanation in the end. The student in charge of feeding this particular group of rabbits liked to fondle and pet them as he worked with them.

Invariably, he would hold each rabbit lovingly for a few minutes before feeding it; astonishingly this alone enabled the animals to resist the toxic diet.

Not very scientific on the face of it, but the scientists there repeated the experiments time and again. And guess what? They came up with the same results.

It goes to show, doesn't it, that it's not what you're eating that really matters, but rather what's eating you.

As Mother Teresa said: "Kindness is a language we all understand. Even the blind can see it and the deaf can hear it."

The philosopher Aldous Huxley was asked on his deathbed about the great life lessons he had learned. He replied in one sentence, one lesson: "It's astonishing to say that after a lifetime of studying the human condition, all I can say is try to be a little bit more kind."

So today is a day to get on the Green Platform, discover your gifts and talents and find a way to use them in the service of humanity. Dr Schweitzer also understood that when you discover your gifts and talents and use them at the service of humanity, happiness is the by-product. He also gave us a great short summary of life on the Green Platform: "I don't know what your destiny will be, but one thing I do know is this: the only ones among you who will be really happy are those who have sought and found how to serve."

Certainly George Bernard Shaw would agree with Dr Schweitzer: "This is the true joy in life, the being used for a purpose recognized by yourself as a mighty one; being a force of nature instead of a feverish selfish clod of ailments and grievances complaining that the world will not devote itself to making you happy.

"I am of the opinion that my life belongs to the whole community and as long as I live it is my privilege to do for it whatever I can.

"I want to be thoroughly used up when I die, for the harder I work, the more I live.

"I rejoice in life for its own sake. Life is no 'brief candle' to me.

It is sort of a splendid torch which I have a hold of for the moment, and I want to make it burn as brightly as possible before handing it over to future generations."

When you use your gifts in the service of others, you really begin to realise and appreciate the real Green Platform truth about yourself and others, no matter how beautiful it may be.

Is there a part of the brain that we can use to get us on to the Green Platform? There is. We've seen it already and how it worked on our Self-Image. It's the Gatekeeper RAS, the Reticular Activating System. It's a powerful tool to get us on to the Green Platform once we know how to use it properly.

CHAPTER 17

RAS – The Gatekeeper To Your Subconscious

THERE is an old Irish saying: "Feiceann súil gruama, saol gruama," which translated means … 'The gloomy eye sees a gloomy world.' It is so true that we see what we want to see; yet the surprising thing is that most of us choose the "suil gruama" (the gloomy eye) approach to our life.

The choice is so simple and yet so hard. All we have to do is to ask empowering questions on the Green Platform or supply our brain with empowering words or visions to spur us on. It's at the centre of what is happening to us; we just have to realise the importance of always going down the 'empowering' route. It is easier said than done though. For some reason, we often default to the disempowering Red Platform side, because it is the one we are used to; it's the one we are more comfortable on.

How does that happen… that we opt to be unhappy and un-abled on the Red Platform rather than be joyful and empowered on the Green Platform? The world inside our heads is very like the inner workings of a computer. We have about eight million pieces of information coming at us from our surroundings at any given time, and there is a real need for a thought strainer or filter. Otherwise it becomes a case where we are totally overwhelmed by the sheer volume of thought-items cascading towards us like a Niagara waterfall. Normally, we would drown under such a deluge.

So there has to be some type of sorting system. Something that will separate the important from the non-important, the significant from the insignificant as we view or understand it.

This is where your Gatekeeper (Reticular Activating System) RAS rides in like John Wayne to save the day for us as we saw when we were looking at the power of our Self-Image to boost or belittle our lives. Let's take a look at it again and what it does.

Your Gatekeeper RAS is a small network of neurons at the back of your brain but it acts as that filter or strainer. It takes in and then sorts all the stimuli coming at you from your surroundings and places them either into the "important bin" or the "rubbish bin." It determines what you will notice and what you will not pay attention to. It acts like a sentry at the door of your mind.

Your conscious mind can only focus on a limited number of elements at one time. Which means that your brain spends a lot of time pushing down the 'delete' button. It works in the background of our existence, making sense of what we do and do not want, having first taken cognisance of our feelings, interpretations etc. In fact it is true to say that this independent republic inside of us all – our Gatekeeper RAS – is responsible for how much or how little of reality we experience in any given minute, in a given hour and in a given day.

It makes the decision on what it will let in and what it will block. Obviously it is programmed to allow in anything that matches your current Self-Image, beliefs and your written goals.

It has a very important function in our life and it is sometimes hard to fathom how acutely aware it is on our behalf. For instance, a mother sleeping at night does not hear cars passing or music from the loud neighbours next door, but a tiny cry from her baby's room and she is suddenly wide awake.

Her Gatekeeper RAS has developed the instinct inside to know that the sound of her baby transcends the other sounds. It is more important and therefore instantly recognisable.

The other stuff is in the background and our Gatekeeper RAS helps us cope with it by selecting the deletion button. Similarly a mother will come to pick up her child from a kindergarten. Out of the all the shouting children she will hear the voice of her own child from outside the door. Her Gatekeeper Reticular Activating System lets it in.

You get a new car and suddenly you see others like it all around you. These types of cars were always there but you never saw them. It had no significance until you bought one and suddenly your Gatekeeper RAS is not deleting this particular piece of information anymore.

We are all the same. Tailors tend to see only the cut of suits. Dentists see the good and the bad in teeth. Farmers see how thin or well-defined cattle are out in a field as they drive by. Someone from a non-farming background will only see the cattle as background, like a hill or a cluster of trees.

Artists see landscapes and cloudscapes. Writers see words; filmmakers see scenes in the everyday for their next movie. All the time the Gatekeeper RAS is in all of these people, busy filtering out what isn't of interest and highlighting what is.

Your Gatekeeper RAS is like a doorman who knows what guests to let in and what ones to send away.

I like to bet with whoever's in a car with me that parking is Gatekeeper RAS related. You know the problem, as you are looking for a parking space in a shopping centre, at a train station or at an airport. We compete with all the other motorists for that valuable place.

You say to yourself: "It's very busy today. I'll never get parking." Then you shut down your Gatekeeper RAS and activate the scotoma or blindness effect where something is in front of you, like the salt on the table that you don't see either.

You almost wish yourself out of a parking spot.

Now I'm the opposite in this regard. I'm the optimist in this case and I always announce to whoever is with me that as I drive in, there are forces at work preparing a spot for me to park in. Of course, it doesn't always happen but I can say this truthfully – I have found in my experience that the more I expect a parking place for me, the more I tend to find one.

It's a little Eureka moment when suddenly you'll spot that puff of smoke coming from the exhaust of a car that's about to leave and you are only too willing to hold up, let the motorists out ahead of you and then triumphantly drive into the empty parking space.

I have a friend who explained that after hearing me speak about this at one of my Green Platform seminars, his Gatekeeper RAS had become part of his weekly life when he was lecturing at a third level institution. Building work at the college car park left vacant slots at a premium.

Whenever he drove towards the place and felt he would serendipitously find a spot, he invariably got one. At times where he felt the law of averages would work against him, he would cruise around for half an hour and then drive off down the town to park in the hotel car park half a mile away.

Over the 13-week term, he found a parking spot 10 times, which he considered way above the average, and admitted the three times he didn't were days when he felt "the world was against me before I even got into the car to head for college."

On a broader level, your Gatekeeper RAS gives you an immediate and heightened awareness of something that has always been around you.

This shift in focus and mental posture aligns you precisely with your goals. Once you decide that something is a clear goal, a priority, and you give it tremendous emotional intensity with positive affirmations or Green Platform Power Talk by continually focusing on it ... then any resource that supports its realisation will turn almost miraculously to help you achieve that aim.

You will become aware of the things you need, to achieve your goal. You will find that you attract the people, the resources and the opportunities to help you reach your goal. Which brings us back to first base. First and foremost you must set your goals, and for that you need a crystal clear 'Why,' a purpose, or a reason.

You say: "I am going back to study because I am getting that qualification by the time I'm 40."

Or you might say: "I am running four times a week to lose 10 pounds within three months." Or you might have an even bigger goal: "I am writing that book I've been talking about for years, only this time I will have a first draft by March 1 next year."

All great stuff.

You have not only identified what and why you want something, but thrown in a 'when' as well. That helps define even better for your Gatekeeper RAS the goals you want to achieve. It will look after the 'how' and sometimes it can appear as if it is happening by chance or coincidence. Sychronicity is what Jung called it – the experience of two or more events as meaningfully related, whereas they are unlikely to be causally related.

Your Gatekeeper RAS will magnetically attract, as I've already mentioned, all the necessary things you need to achieve your goal.

You see once you move, once you take action in the direction of your goals, then the great hand of Providence moves as well to help too. It's like beginning a journey where you walk down a long corridor with many doors. Until you move, no door will open. Firstly you must start moving. Then and only then will the doors open. If you take all the actions, then the law of attraction will do the rest. When you move, Providence moves too.

So what's stopping you?

Just as an empowering mentality on the Green Platform will allow you change your life and hit new goals, a disempowering attitude on the Red Platform will pull the rug from under your feet before you get started.

You could hear yourself say: "Get a degree! You were lucky to pass your Leaving Cert."

Or: "I've always had problems with my weight and I've always failed to get any thinner."

Or maybe worst of all: "Would you cop yourself on. You write a book? You can hardly write your name."

That's all it takes for you to turn against the chance of reinventing yourself and enjoying the new challenges you set yourself. A negative belittling remark. There's one certainty in life – a disempowering question on the Red Platform will guarantee a disempowering answer.

Always.

Your Gatekeeper RAS will only let in all the evidence to make your question the truth as you see it.

Now flip the coin.

If you jump on The Green Platform and ask yourself an empowering questions like: "How can I achieve this new goal and enjoy the process?" then your Gatekeeper RAS will start the hunt and leave no stone unturned to help you do what you want.

It will initiate searches for all the ways, and people, and opportunities to turn this around and it will always look for opportunities to enjoy the process. The subconscious loves a challenge that it can tackle. And by presenting it in this way, that's exactly what you have given it.

Your empowering question will open your Gatekeeper RAS door to let this situation hit the high priority levels on your daily list. It's like buying that unusual car and you think this is the only one in the world, and then you see similar versions all over the place. The fact is that they were always there but before you tuned in your Gatekeeper RAS, there was no real reason to notice them.

This is why as we've seen, it is so critical for you to have a strong positive Self-Image on the Green Platform. Then your RAS will let in everything to reinforce that image.

It is important to know that it works the other way too.

If you have a negative belittling Self-Image, then your Gatekeeper RAS will let in everything to reinforce that negative Self-Image and ensure that you continue to live on that toxic Red Platform.

It will be a magnet pulling in and attracting all the nasty stuff that will prove you right to have a negative Self-Image.

So where do you stand as you read this? The chances are you will favour the Red Platform: "I can't do it."

If you agree with my assessment, don't feel bad about it. Most of us are defaulted to doubt ourselves. So you are no different.

Where the difference comes in is when you choose to leave that platform and switch to The Green Platform where you don't just say "I can do it", but actually believe you can do it.

Your Gatekeeper RAS is a powerful tool to help you achieve your dreams and goals. First we need a dream, a castle in the air. Then we'll put legs and foundations under it and let your Gatekeeper RAS go to work.

CHAPTER 18

GOAL
Finding Your Dream And Following It

WE had the agricultural age. Then the industrial age. Now we're just emerged from the "information age" to the age of stories, rituals, imagination, symbolism, authentic experiences and spiritual growth. There is a massive difference between information and inspiration. In terms of change, growth and achieving our dreams, information is important, but it's not enough. Information alone falls far short.

The information on the back of a cigarette packet says "Smoking kills." That is pretty chilling news but the human psyche has the capacity to take such a warning in, totally ignore the information and then proceed to light up. That's because information is a left-brain linear thing. Information alone will never do it for us. Otherwise we would not have obese doctors or grumpy psychologists or seriously negative and sad priests and ministers. If information did it for us then customer care would replace customer contempt.

We need inspiration to drive us on. Inspiration means to "breathe spirit into." Inspiration is an emotional or a spiritual component. To be inspired, we need a powerful magnetic dream or vision. Happy are those who dream dreams and are willing to do whatever it takes (without hurting anyone) and enjoy the journey to making them happen.

Around 250 BC Patangeli understood clearly this difference between information and inspiration. He said:

"When You Are Inspired
By Some Great Purpose
Some Extraordinary Project

All Your Thoughts Break Their Bonds
Your Mind Transcends Limitations
Your Consciousness Expands in Every Direction
And You Find Yourself In A New and A Great
and A Wonderful World
Dormant Forces, Faculties and Talents Come Alive
And You Discover Yourself To Be A Greater Person By Far
Than You Ever Dreamed Yourself To Be!"

Notice the first line. Patangeli said, when you are "inspired." He didn't say, "informed" by some great purpose.

The American essayist and philosopher Ralph Waldo Emerson was a great believer in the human race. He felt we had a lot more to offer the world than we realised. He suggested: "Do not follow where the path may lead. Go instead where there is no path and leave a trail."

To be inspired we need a great purpose, an extraordinary project or a dream that will inspire us to start the journey on the path where there is no trail. When people make great movies or great actors win Oscars, they often talk about the burning desire, the fire in the belly, the dream or vision they had which drove them on to such pinnacles. How do you discover or find your dream? Perhaps it might be good to start with daydreaming. Like Albert Einstein.

Albert recalls how his first insight that would lead to his Theory of Relativity came to him unexpectedly. He was just a 16-year-old and he was daydreaming.

"What would it be like," Einstein asked himself, "to run beside a light beam at the speed of light?" You can see why he believed that imagination was more important than knowledge. He was also dreaming a big dream. If you are going to dream, then do it in style and in grand manner.

Once that dream was embedded in his brain, the great man continually revisited it and it became a major part of his imagination. He housed the vision in his head as if it was real.

It is important to remember that as he progressed to imagine himself riding on a beam of light and holding a mirror up to his face to see what might be happening, he was constantly being told by classical physics that he would see nothing.

Light would have to travel faster than the light beam he was travelling on to allow him see himself. Einstein's instinct could not accept this was true and for years afterwards he went about proving mathematically that his instinct was right.

Now here's the thing. Einstein's inspiration came from allowing himself to dream. Daydreaming gives you the opportunity not just to think outside the box but also to imagine there never was a box in the first place. You cannot read the label on the jar when you are standing inside the jar. As Michelangelo said: "The problem is not that our dreams are too big and we don't reach them, it's that they are too small and we do reach them."

While we may not do anything as amazing as Einstein's theory of relativity we can still have a vision or dream. Then the inspiration inside will light the fire of burning desire to carry it through. Just being inspired by a big dream is a great way to change your life.

Ask yourself what does your dream of excellence look like? What would your ideal day look like? Sound like? Feel like? Try to get a clear picture of your vision. See if you can create a vision board and put pictures of your dream on it.

Some time ago I worked with a client on the Green Platform Goal Achieving blueprint. One of his dreams was to own a Mercedes. So on the first page he put a picture of his dream driving machine. Within a month he saw his exact car at half the original price and as he drove away from the garage, he told me he kept asking himself: "Would it have happened anyway if I hadn't put the vision picture on the first page?"

Did he magnetically attract it by focusing clearly and vividly on what he wanted? Or did it just fortunately happen as his desire to have one intensified? What do you think? Is there something to it or is it just a coincidence and it's pure baloney to read anything more into it?

To make a difference we need to put energy batteries under our dreams. These are our values. So ask yourself what are the values that are going to drive my dream?

Integrity? Trust? Work/Life Balance? Environmental Sustainability? Tractability? Dependable? Reliability? Loyal? Committed? Open-mindedness? Consistency? Honesty? Efficiency? Innovative? Creative? Humour? Fun-loving? Adventurous? Motivated? Positive? Optimistic? Inspiring? Passionate? Respectful? Athletic? Fit? Courageous? Educated? Respected? Loving?

Clarifying your values is often the starting point to high achievement and peak performance. Living in alignment with your true values is the only road to self-confidence, self-respect and personal pride. In fact, almost every major corporate problem over the past few decades came from companies being out of alignment with their true values. When corruption, incompetence and cronyism replace trust, integrity and contribution bad things happen and huge numbers of people suffer. When we start stuffing horsemeat into hamburgers to make a quick small profit, then that invisible value called trust is broken. The cost? Millions and millions of euros plus thousands of jobs lost.

There's little point in having your values written out and up on a plaque on a wall if you haven't inspiring stories that illustrate each value. Only when the value has a real living story wrapped around it does it come to life for the people in the company or organisation.

Alltech, the health and nutrition company that sponsors the Alltech World Equestrian Games has a number of corporate values. One of them is contribution or social responsibility. This value has generated so many powerful inspiring stories.

When the tsunami hit South East Asia they didn't just give money. Their people went there. Lived with the people. They built 12 boats, five schools and a store. They got to know the people face to face on a personal level as they worked with them side by side helping them to rebuild their lives.

When the earthquake hit Haiti, they went there and bought coffee from a co-operative of 6,700 farmers, sold it as Alltech Citadelle Coffee and all the profits went to the poor coffee farmers. They also built a school and are in the process of building a rum distillery to provide jobs and create sustainable development.

They don't believe in just handouts except in extraordinary circumstances. It's more about hand-ups. It's about empowering and enabling people to be independent, self-sustaining and self-nourishing. They don't want to feed the world. They want to enable the world to have the power and ability to feed themselves and their animals nutritious and nourishing food, not junk food. They do not want to create more malnourished fat people like we have in the so-called developed nations.

The key thing here is that "contribution," or "social responsibility" isn't just a value on a plaque on a corporate wall. It's a core value with Alltech that comes alive in and through the people with all the stories it generates. What brings this value and other values alive and off the plaque are the stories that people tell about the value.

A number of Alltech employees climbed the famous Kilimanjaro Mountain in Africa and raised a huge amount of money for sustainable development projects in Haiti. No one told them to do it. They took the initiative themselves. They were inspired. Stories bring the values alive. Values on a plaque without inspiring stories are impotent and have no power to touch people's hearts and minds and souls and inspire action.

The next challenge in living our dream is to break our dream down into Fiercely Important Goals (FIGS). The big ones, the quantum leap ones that matter most and will be the difference that makes the difference.

CHAPTER 19

GOAL
So How Are Your FIGs
(Fiercely Important Goals)?

A DREAM will remain a dream unless we break it down into clear realistic but stretching goals. To achieve any dream you will always have three FIGs. These are the ones that will help you achieve your dream faster, more efficiently and more effectively than anything else. First let's take a look at goals in general.

As we have seen in earlier chapters, there is so much information circulating around in our heads at any given time that it is impossible for us to remember or even understand it all, much less make sense of a small percentage of it.

There are ways, though, which help us to highlight the information we would like to prioritise in our lives. Let's focus on that for a little while now.

Goals and Goal-Setting has become such a cliché in modern parlance that they have lost much of their meaning. Certainly that is the case as a valuable day-to-day tool to help us attain what we want to achieve.

Goals are like cars; if we used them properly, they can drive us to where we want to go. What, though, if the car always has a flat battery when we want to go to work or only has three tyres pumped up? We would quickly see that a car in such a condition is really of little help to us at all in getting to work, driving to school or in going to see a football game.

Similarly what passes for Goals in much of today's writings are no more than instant reminders. Unfortunately, these in turn are instantly forgotten as we go about our multi-tasking day. They have as much chance of working as a car with no battery or with a flat tyre.

We have Red Platform goals and Green Platform goals. Red Platform goals are vague, wooly, fuzzy, and abstract. Green Platform goals are specific, measurable, realistic but stretching, rewarding and time-bound, not just in a To-Do list, but in your diary.

"To lose weight," is a Red Platform goal. Why? Because it's vague, woolly and fuzzy.

"To lose seven pounds by November 30th is a Green Platform goal." It is specific, measurable, attainable, realistic, stretching, and it has a date, a time.

Green Platform goals have to be realistic but stretching for you. For instance if you are throwing darts at a dart board, and you walk up to within a foot of the dart board, you can put your dart straight into the bull's eye. Not much of a challenge there. But if you go back 50 yards, your dart will not even reach the dartboard. There is a right distance that is realistic, but stretching and challenging.

It's the same with Green Platform stretching goals.

Be specific or as specific as you can be at the start of this great goal-setting odyssey you are undertaking. Measurable means measurable in space and time – "How much and by when?"

I will have two chapters of my book written by August 31st or I will apply to do that course or degree immediately and finish it by 2015.

Once you do that, it is no longer a wishy-washy thought flowing through your head. There is meat and drink to what you are planning.

For instance, if you were to tell me that you wanted more money to improve your lifestyle, I could take a euro out of my pocket and give it to you. You would probably protest, saying: "No, I meant a lot more money, like €100,000 or a million euro."

It is important that you define "more money" so that I can understand exactly what you want.

As soon as you commit to a big dream and go after it, and write it down, your subconscious, creative mind will come up with big ideas to help you make it happen. Just like it did with our friend Albert Einstein.

Big dreams not only inspire you, they compel others to want to dream big too. Our dreams will remain dreams unless we break them down into three FIGS – three Fiercely Important Goals.

Once you have a clear, mental high-definition picture of your FIG, your 'how' begins to emerge as there is momentum gathering that will make it happen.

Like a modern SatNav or GPS system, all you have to do is punch in the destination (write down your FIG) and your subconscious will take you there ... your subconscious will look after the 'how.'

Once you think it and ink it, once you commit your goal to writing, your Gatekeeper RAS door will pull in the people, opportunities and resources to make it happen.

Anyone who ever achieved anything great didn't know how they were going to do it; they just knew they were going to do it.

You'll also discover that when your dreams include service to others, that is, accomplishing something that contributes to mankind, it accelerates the accomplishment of that goal. People want to be part of something that contributes and makes a difference. People today are hungry for purpose and meaning.

Make sure your Green Platform goals are 'ecologically' sound. In other words, who else is going to be involved in your process? Who do you need to get buy-in from? Who do you need to negotiate with?

If your goal is to learn to play golf for four hours every Saturday, have you got the 'all-clear' from your partner, children or elderly parents in a nursing home?

You don't want to hear: "Where do you think you're going with the bag of golf clubs at this time on a Saturday morning and not a child in the house washed or fed?"

Share your goals. Get buy-in from those around you. Negotiate times to suit all concerned.

"I'll take an hour at 10 for a run, and you can play tennis from 12 to two."

Make sure it's a win-win. Mutually beneficial. Real Green Platform goals.

Creating the proper environment to achieve your dream may mean that you may have to change your lifestyle by getting up at 6am instead of 7.30am.

If that's what it takes, you have to make sure you are (quite literally) up for it. If you can get your partner in life to also partner you in your goal, your chances of achieving what you want will have a much greater chance of success.

This is what we call the Green Platform Partner Programme (the GPPP). When you have an accountability partner, a Green Platform Partner, your chances of goal implementation according to the American Association of Training & Development shoots up from 40 per cent to a massive 95 per cent.

Nearly all the great achievers who changed the world had a Green Platform Partner. Walt Disney had Roy Disney, Steve Jobs had Steve Wozniak and Orville Wright had Wilbur Wright.

My friend Dr Pearse Lyons had his friends Nathan Honan and Bill Cheek when he he was building his global company Alltech out of his garage. When his first big order came in, he could have prevaricated and said he would wait until he had a proper premises before trying to sell his products.

He had a philosophy which has turned him into a billionaire – "Don't get it right; get it going!"

He says there is never a time for everything to be 'just right.' If you hide behind that, then the chances are you will never get started. You'll sink in procrastination due to perfectionism. Get it going and then like a heat-seeking missile, you'll self-correct to your goal target as you go along.

There is a lot of merit in that philosophy. The person or the system with the greatest flexibility has the greatest power to change to the proper course.

If something is not working, try something else. If that doesn't work, then try something else again. Above all, don't keep on working harder at something that patently doesn't work.

I'm sure you've heard of the phrase: "Feedback is the breakfast of champions."

So work with whatever tools you have and identify better tools as you go along. The Lyons' principle works because it is always about research, progress and a relentless quest for excellence and quality control. Once he got it going, he made sure everything was right, to the highest possible standard. Once he gets it going, he's obsessed with quality.

In the absence of clearly defined goals, we live on the reactive Red Platform and become strangely loyal to performing daily rubbishy trivia until ultimately we become enslaved by it. Things that matter least take over from things that matter most. Sometimes we can do very well what we should not be doing at all.

Are you like that?

I am.

Or at least I was until it dawned on me that I was sabotaging my own goals by prioritising things to do which were just preventing me from working on what I should be pursuing.

I will give you an example. For maybe two decades now I have been 'promising myself' that I must write a book on The Green Platform, largely as a response to the many people coming up after conferences and asking me if I had a book on the topic to which they had just been introduced.

That sort of marketing feedback is invaluable to any would-be author. I also saw that if I wrote the book, it could be a great help to those people and many more because they would have a reference to use on a daily basis for the rest of their lives if they so wished. That would fulfil a very important component in my goal setting; doing something that might help individuals and the population in general.

Despite those clear signals beaming directly into my reception tower, I prevaricated and then prevaricated some more by putting other writing engagements, magazine columns, articles and conference scripts and PowerPoints ahead of knuckling down to The Green Platform book.

Even when a friend, seeing the book's introduction, came especially to the US with me to discuss writing it three years ago (and events around that visit saw two people approach me as if sent by the hand of Providence,) I came home and continued to talk the talk but didn't walk the book-writing walk.

I must confess I didn't feel great about it and then one day out walking I asked myself would I ever write The Green Platform at all? That realisation stirred something deep inside me and there and then I snapped into Operation Green Platform mindset.

I put this project at the top of my Goal Setting and suddenly things began to fall into place like I've never seen happen before. I was practising what I'd been preaching and I loved every minute of it. My advice was more than that to myself. I decided that I wasn't just getting started for the sake of it but I was going to stay on the right path all the way to the last page.

The turbo power to achieve your goal is your ability to take massive and consistent action and combine that with a powerful "Why?" It's your jet fuel. Eighty per cent of the energy we need for our goal comes from the 'why' – the purpose or the reason.

Once you have that, you are priming yourself up for success.

I put rocket fuel under my goal by writing out three "whys" or three deep-felt reasons for writing this book.

(1) It was something I desperately wanted to do for a long time.

(2) If it was published, it would be available to all the people who had attended my Green Platform seminars but always seemed disappointed that I hadn't a book for them to bring away.

(3) By being on the bookstands, it might just help some people in the general population who had never heard of The Green Platform way of living because it wasn't in bookshops before.

Once I did that, I threw myself headlong into the project and enjoyed every minute of the journey. At last I knew I was being true to myself and to my family and friends and work colleagues by prioritising this as Project No 1 to be achieved.

I broke the book writing dream into three FIGs and started on the first one. The first chapter. Then took it from there. I discovered the truth of Thoreou's statement: "If one advances confidently in the direction of his dreams, and endeavors to live the life that he has imagined, he will meet with a success unexpected in common hours."

CHAPTER 20

GOAL
How The Universe Conspires With You

THOREAU speaks of advancing confidently in the direction of your dreams and then, you will meet with a success unexpected in common hours. It's the world conspiring with you. It's Providence waiting ... waiting ... then moving when you move.

A big part of the enjoyment of writing this book was that when I decided to fully commit to the project, I saw and experienced the universe conspired with me at virtually every turn to make it happen.

This could be called the Road Less Travelled chapter. I've decided to include it because it gives a background to something that is often the centre of criticism by people who do not believe in the theory of the universe conspiring to help us in proper goal-achieving situations.

After decades of research into how the human brain works, scientists now know that for our brains to figure out how to get what we want, we must first decide what we want.

What is your Fiercely Important Goal?

Once you lock-in your FIG, our mind and the universe can step in to help make our dreams a reality by attracting the people, resources, circumstances and opportunities to achieve and exceed your written goals.

We are part of an enormous bowl of energy soup that is the Universe. We have cells, then atoms, then subatomic particles and then little waves of information and energy. The neuroscientists now tell us that 99.9 per cent of everything is actually nothing, empty space that is open to the power of intention and attention. In a very real sense what we think about we bring about. We are energy transmitters and receivers. Every thought we think has an energy pulse that resonates. This has a magnetic quality and follows the 'like attracts like' process. So when you think about positive things you can attract more positive things into your life. When you think negative things you literally become a toxic magnet. If you are complaining you will attract more of the things you are complaining about. Whereas if you are focusing on what's positive and what you really want you will attract more of that into your life.

All of creation is related through an unseen force and our inner world influences our outer world through this invisible force. In the 1990s, Western science began to confirm, under laboratory conditions, what ancient texts and metaphysics have been saying for hundreds and hundreds of years: We are, in fact, surrounded by a field of energy that responds to our inner world. Life is not happening to you, it's responding to you.

In the early 1990s, a Russian scientist named Valdimir Poponin conducted an experiment to see if human DNA had an effect on the world around it. Poponin started the experiment by creating a vacuum in a glass tube. Then, he measured the photons, tiny vibrating particles of light, and determined that they were randomly scattered throughout the tube. As you may already know, our world is made of photons. Although you can remove air from an enclosed space, seemingly it's impossible to remove the photons.

Next, the researchers placed human DNA in the tube to see if it had any effect on the photons.

And guess what?

The photons abandoned their random pattern and aligned themselves along the axis of the DNA.

Adapting his study to these findings, Poponin later removed the DNA from the tube to see if the photons would fall back to their original pattern. They didn't; instead they remained ordered as if the DNA were still there.

In a second related experiment, the Institute of HeartMath tested to see if isolated DNA would respond to changes in emotion.

In this case, the researchers used a group of people who had been trained to generate coherent emotions at will. They were trained to feel compassion, love, or forgiveness on command. And they could turn that emotion around and feel anger, hate, or jealousy at the drop of a hat.

The experiments were designed to determine the specific effects different emotions had on DNA, and what in turn that might mean in our bodies.

The scientists found that when in the presence of such emotions as understanding, compassion, and appreciation, the twin strands of DNA began to relax and elongate. And when in the presence of negative emotions, the DNA strands tightened up.

What's particularly interesting about this is that the researchers found when DNA is relaxed and elongated, the body is better able to heal itself.

The United States Army Intelligence and Security Command (INSCOM) performed this experiment in the nineties. This time the researchers took DNA from donors and placed it in a device that can measure changes in DNA.

The DNA samples were placed in one room while the donor was placed in another room of the same building. The donor was then shown humorous videos or images of graphic violence to elicit emotional responses.

And what they discovered is that when the donor was having an emotional response, his DNA, which was in another room, was having a response in the very same instant.

Now conventional wisdom tells us that somehow the donor's emotions were transmitted from one room to another – similar to the way a television signal is transmitted across space. But when you transmit energy, typically it takes time to get from point A to point B. In other words, there's a lag time. But, in the INSCOM experiment, there was no lag time.

The researchers decided to take things a step further to see just how far these effects occurred. So they separated the DNA and the donor by as much as 400 miles. Amazingly, the results were duplicated – there was still no lag time.

We've seen that science has proven that 99.9 per cent of your body is empty space – just a bunch of atoms whirling around in a big field of nothingness. But this empty space is the interesting part about you. According to Dr. Deepak Chopra, it's in this emptiness that you'll find everything that sustains life. Everything shares the same field of pure energy. Even though you can't see it, or touch it, this field of pure energy is there.

But what's really amazing about this field of energy is what makes it move. What do you think makes energy move?

According to Dr. Chopra, it's 'thought' that moves the energy. He explains: "This field of so-called nothingness that fills 99.9 per cent of you and makes up 99.9 per cent of everything in the universe is energy and intelligence. Just little waves of information and energy. This is why thought can move it."

This is also why intention matters. Your intention really matters. "Thought moves energy." For better or worse.

So in summary, when you think positive thoughts and feel positive feelings on the Green Platform, you attract more positive things into your life. When you think negative thoughts and feel negative feelings you attract more negative things into your life. What you think about expands and moves your energy, for better or for worse.

When you move Providence moves too and it will move in the direction or your thoughts. The mountain climber W.H. Murray highlighted this idea very well by claiming that when you make a bold commitment to do something, Providence moves too.

He explained: "...that until one is committed, there is hesitancy, the chance to draw back, always ineffectiveness. Concerning all acts of initiative (and creation), there is one elementary truth the ignorance of which kills countless ideas and splendid plans: that the moment one definitely commits oneself, then Providence moves too.

A whole stream of events issues from the decision, raising in one's favour all manner of unforeseen incidents, meetings and material assistance, which no man could have dreamt would have come his way. I have a deep respect for one of Goethe's couplets:

Whatever you can do or dream you can, begin it.

Boldness has genius, power and magic in it."

Tap in your three FIGs into your internal SatNav and your dreams will come true if you have the courage to pursue them with total, consistent and persistent commitment.

Commitment to do what we'll say we'll do, long after the mood in which we said it is gone. Private victories always come before public victories.

Then you become an inverse paranoid by constantly expecting the world to support you, to bring you marvellous opportunities and to do you good.

There are those who ask: "What happened?"

There are those who watch things happen.

Then there are those on the Green Platform who make things happen and at the same time allow things to happen. Does life happen to you on the Red Platform or are you happening to life?

It's like the story of the hen and the pig discussing commitment one sunny afternoon in the shade of a tree. The question they were discussing was: "How committed are you?"

"Well," said the hen, "I'm very committed. I provide the farmer with eggs for the family breakfast every morning."

"That's nothing," said the pig. "I'm totally committed, I provide the bacon."

Be a creator on the Green Platform, not a victim on the Red Platform. Make things happen. Then watch for the signs and omens and allow things to happen. Go for your dream. Get on the Green Platform and follow your bliss. Follow the true north of your own personal inner compass. Then watch the universe conspire with you to make it happen. You will meet with "a success unexpected in common hours."

Robert Kennedy put it well: "There are those who look at things the way they are and ask why ... I dream things that never were and ask why not?"

To make your dreams of things that never were manifest into reality, to achieve and exceed your FIGs, you'll need to get a good start. You'll need focus and clarity, you'll need to keep the whole process very simple and you'll accelerate the achievement of your Fiercely Important Goals when you build in some powerful good habits into your life.

That's your next challenge.

CHAPTER 21

GOAL
A Beginning,
Middle And End

AMERICAN management guru and statistician W. Edwards Deming established the Total Quality Movement (TQM), first in Japan at a time when "Made in Japan" signalled shoddy goods. Then he established it throughout the world.

Deming's contribution is historically so important that the US News and World Report called him one of the nine hidden turning points of history (along with the birth control pill and the apostle Paul).

After 50 years of statistical study, Deming pointed out that in every process there is a beginning, a middle and an end.

When you focus on the first 15 per cent of that process, and get it correct (its initial conditions), you ensure at least 85 per cent of the desired outcome.

By focusing on the first 15 per cent of anything, the remaining 85 per cent will effortlessly follow.

The best way to get things correct in the first 15 per cent is to keep things simple.

In 1142, William of Ockham, a British philosopher, proposed a method of problem solving that has come to be referred to as 'Ockham's Razor.' What Ockham said was: "The simplest and most direct solution, requiring the fewest number of steps, is usually the correct solution to any problem."

Many people make the mistake of over-complicating goals and problems. But the more complicated the solution, the less likely it is ever to be implemented, and the longer the time it will take to get any results.

Your aim with your goal setting on the Green Platform should be to simplify the solution and go directly to the goal, as quickly as possible.

As Charles Mingus said: "Anyone can make the simple complicated but making the complicated simple, stunningly simple – that's creativity."

Warren Buffet concurred: "The business schools reward difficult complex behaviour, but simple behaviour is more effective." When Albert Einstein was asked what was the secret of his scientific success he replied: "Keep it simple. Make it fun."

The first simple step is to write down what your goal is. If you think it, ink it. By doing this, you are beginning the journey to achievement. When you write down a goal, it is the first signal as to what direction you intend to travel. You are alerting clearly to yourself amidst all the traffic in your mind that there is a signpost ahead which you must follow.

Your FIGs start to manifest the second you write them down. Just get them out of your head and onto paper. People who write goals are 10 times more likely to achieve them than those who don't.

You also need to attach a compelling, emotionally-charged picture so that it becomes a 'special project' for your mind to focus on. You need to get it marked 'top priority' by your Gatekeeper RAS. As we already saw, once we make this a centrepiece of our daily action, we attract the people, opportunities, ideas and resources to turn our goal into reality.

Take a little leap of faith when you are in the process of achieving a goal. Envisage the feeling you will get from the fulfilled goal before it actually happens. Then detach from the outcome. Don't keep saying: "I wonder will this really work?" It is already working as the journey gets under way. You are open to everything and attached to nothing while on your way. Then try to be grateful at every stage of the goal achieving process. Gratitude is one of our most powerful emotions we have to attract back a matching vibration from the universe. Then even more than before your Gatekeeper RAS will welcome your goal and process it.

FOCUS AND CLARITY

So to make our dream come true, we need to write down three FIGs – Fiercely Important Goals to ensure they get 'Top Priority Clearance'. Your Gatekeeper RAS will then welcome them and activate the implementation process. They need to be highly visible. We need daily reminders of what these goals are, why they are top priority so that our Gatekeeper RAS will welcome them and get out subconscious working on the 'how' of achieving them.

Now I want to draw your attention to a Harris Poll, where 150,000 people across 1,100 companies were interviewed. They were asked this question... 'in your company, what are the top three company goals?'

It might surprise you that 85 per cent hadn't a clue what was being asked of them, never mind understanding the concept of gilt-edging goals to make them stand out. What a massive dissipation of energy. Not a goal signpost in sight. So only 15 per cent had an idea what was going on and knew the top three company goals.

They were asked a follow-up question: 'How is your job connected to making these top three goals happen.'

By also bringing the workplace into it, the amount of people who hadn't a clue jumped to 94 per cent, meaning a miniscule six per cent were clued in. Only six per cent could see the connection between their daily work and its alignment with the top three goals.

That's why we need a highly visible scoreboard to keep us totally focused on achieving our FIGs. Our continual internal question is always: "Is this activity getting me near my FIG or farther away from my FIG?"

I've never seen a game of football or hurling or basketball or baseball during my lifetime without a massive scoreboard bringing instant update to everyone involved with the process. Progress in the game is measured consistently and is highly visible.

It's rare, however, that we see our own personal lives or company scoreboards displayed in such a fashion. That is a pity because what we are doing here is measuring what we are doing.

And "what gets measured gets managed and gets done", was another of Demings' great insights.

All this takes loads of energy to keep going. Where, you might well ask, do I get energy for these Goals?

If I have a clear, high-definition picture of my dream or goal or outcome on the Green Platform and also have an absolute clear picture of now, current reality – between those pictures, there is a gap.

Now there is a huge vortex of energy in that gap – if the goal is clear and focused. So for implementation here, clarity and focus are key. If however the goal is a vague, fuzzy, woolly, abstract Red Platform goal, then there is very little energy to achieve anything.

Clarity and focus are the key to all goal implementation. If I take a world champion archer and put myself up against him in an archery contest, how can I guarantee you that I will beat him – after about one hour's training.

We put him 50 feet from the target, then blindfold him, turn him around and around and let him stop wherever he likes.

We ask him to shoot. The question he asks us is: "How can I hit a target that I cannot see?"

Good question, Mr Archer. That's the question for us to ask ourselves too. If we can't see the target, how can we come near to hitting it? Goals are our targets but we must be able to see them clearly if we are to hit them.

Remember those 85 per cent who hadn't a clue what the three company FIGs were? How could they possibly help to achieve them or have any hope of measuring their success?

If I hold a dry leaf in my hand and hold it all afternoon in the sun, nothing will happen to it. If I get a magnifying glass and focus the light of the sun on it, it will kindle and blaze up ... it is the same light except that it is focused to a thousandth degree.

The light in a light bulb is the same energy as the light in a laser beam which can cut through steel, except the laser beam is focused, and that's the key difference.

Focus and clarity are key to goal achieving on the Green Platform.

I remember doing a Goal Achievement Review with a European manager some time ago. He showed me his goals. "You didn't achieve this one," I said.

"No I didn't but how did you know?" he asked.

"By the way you wrote it."

Here's what he had written.

"To write articles for magazines about our products."

Of course it never happened. Then he asked me: "How will I write it so that it will happen?"

"Well, the first thing is you get it off your To-Do List and into your diary. Put in your diary that from 8 am to 11 am on Thursday next you will write this article on this product for this particular editor. Have it finished by 11.00. Emailed to the editor by 11.01 and then final feedback at 12.00 noon. Then your article will be not only written but printed. If it's a top priority you make it a top priority. During that time you do nothing else. No phone calls. No emails. No texts. No tweets. No social media postings. Just total focus on writing your article."

That's how you write and achieve a goal on the Green Platform.

There's a difference between being efficient and being effective.

Efficient is 'doing the thing right.' You can be very efficient cutting down trees in a wood.

Effective is 'doing the right thing.' Are you in the right wood, or should you be in the wood at all?

For every task, ask yourself: "Am I doing this in the most efficient way? In the most effective way? Is this really necessary? Am I the appropriate person to be doing this?

There is an extraordinary time in your life when you are actually doing something you were put on this earth to do. Following your bliss. This is what you're truly brilliant at, your core genius. For Michelangelo it was sculpting, not doing accounts. The poet W.H. Auden put his finger on these moments when people are really following their bliss, doing what they were born to do, lined up with their own inner true north, and using their talents on the Green Platform in the service of humanity. His poem is called Mastery:

"You need to see what someone is doing
To know if it is their vocation
You have only to watch his eyes:
A cook mixing a sauce, a surgeon
Making a primary incision
A clerk completing a bill of lading,
Wear the same rapt expression, forgetting
Themselves in function.
How beautiful it is,
That eye-on-object look."

"Forgetting themselves in function ...how beautiful it is that eye-on-object look."

Isn't that a marvellous description of someone doing what they were born to do? Mozart playing the piano. Someone baking bread or a farmer mowing a field of hay.

If you want to discover a real conveyor belt for goal achievement, then build good habits. The Green Platform is the home of good habits. The Red Platform is the home of bad habits. Good habits are hard to develop and easy to let go. Bad habits are easy to develop and hard to let go.

Aristotle once said: "Excellence is not an act, but a habit." The poet John Dryden added significantly to that by stating: "We first make our habits and then our habits make us."

The old Chinese proverb is something worth remembering as you begin to form your habits on the road to achieving your goals. "Habits are cobwebs at first; cables at last."

What is a habit? Authors John J. Murphy and Mac Anderson in their book 'Habits Die Hard' reference a poem that gives a great insight into habits:

"I am your constant companion
I am your greatest asset or your heaviest burden.
I will push you up to success or down to disappointment.
Half the things you do are from me.
I am easily managed; just be firm with me
Those who are great, I have made great.
Those who are failures, I have made failures.
I am not a machine, though I work with the precision of a
machine and the intelligence of a person.
You can run me for profit, or you can run me for ruin.
Show me how you want it done.
Educate me.
Train me.
Lead me.
Reward me.
And I will then...do it automatically.
I am your servant.
Who am I?
I am a habit."

It takes 28 days to embed one for good. The thing about a good habit is that most of us stop after 24 or 26 days, just when it's about to be embedded.

If you want to change a habit, here's the seven Green Platform steps you need to take:

1. Make a note of the habit you want to change.

2. Write down what your aim is in changing the habit. This will help to clarify your motive – motivation.

3. Give yourself a precise time.

4. List all the disadvantages of your bad habits.

5. List the advantages of changing. Build in rewards for every breakthrough. I'm a week off cigarettes. How will I celebrate?

6. Exaggerate a little at the beginning, like arriving always 15 minutes early for appointments.

7. Involve other people. Get a positive encouraging Green Platform Accountability Partner who will totally support you.

The habit of organised and disciplined goal setting and achieving on the Green Platform will carry you easily through life's toughest times.

To dream things that never were and achieve them, to have that burning desire and passion to see possibility, to follow your bliss and your own true north on your inner compass doing what you were born to do, to achieve and exceed your FIGs, you must be working and living out of your strengths. Now we'll look at the power of working out of your strengths rather than spending a lost lifetime fixing your weaknesses. That means for Mozart to work our his natural talent and strength to be a better pianist and composer, rather than being out in the milking shed trying to fix his cow-milking weaknesses.

CHAPTER 22

GOAL
Strengths On
The Green Platform

IF you are working out of your strengths, you are much more likely to achieve your Green Platform Goals. When you are working out of your weaknesses, you are definitely on the Red Platform.

In a Gallup poll some time ago employees were asked how they were using their strengths in the service of their company. Only 20 per cent said they were using their strengths to the full. In a follow-up poll some time later, people were again asked about how the company was using their strengths.

This time only 17 per cent said the company was using them properly, playing to their strengths. That means in terms of untapped potential in companies, there is 83 per cent of untapped potential. So many people working out of their weaknesses or their non-strengths if you like.

So in terms of work productivity we have 17 per cent engaged and working productively out of their strengths on the Green Platform, and 83 per cent floundering and struggling in their weaknesses on the Red Platform.

It seems most managers are massively committed to teaching hens how to swim. And they are probably working very hard at it. For three hours in the morning they work extremely hard at teaching the hen to swim. Still the hen is useless at swimming. Then they build a hen gym (They're totally committed to helping, enabling and empowering this hen to swim) and work on the hen's swimming muscles for three hours every afternoon in the gym. They even hire a personal trainer to monitor the hen's gym work measuring muscle twitch, heartbeat and every other measurable function. Then I'm called in. Get her off the Red Platform and get her thinking positively on the Green Platform.

"Do some Self-Image work with the hen. Tell her the hen you see is the hen you'll be."

"Okay."

"All you need is belief, hen. Get on the Green Platform, hen. You're spending your swimming life on the Red Platform."

Still the hen is no good at swimming. Then they give the hen her PDR, her Personal Development Review. They share the 360 degree feedback with the hen. "It's not just me," says the manager, "but everyone else says your swimming is very poor and you need to work hard and improve your swimming."

The hen leaves utterly depressed and fed up. Demotivated. The manager is utterly frustrated. He couldn't be working harder. He wonders whether the hen ever listens to a word he says. "I might as well be talking to the wall," he mutters.

Then one day they discover a duck. Hey presto, the duck swims and all they have to do is empower the duck to be a better swimmer. The hen is moved to laying eggs and becomes supremely good in her own area of excellence. Now she's laying more eggs. She's a happy hen. She's following her bliss. She's working out of her strengths on the Green Platform. So is the duck. And so is the manager.

The lessons for managers everywhere from this little story is:

On the Green Platform we are teaching ducks to swim and hens to lay eggs. On the Red Platform we are teaching hens to swim.

On the Green Platform we build strengths, we teach ducks to be better swimmers. It's not about working harder, it's about working smarter. On the Red Platform we fix weaknesses. We work harder at what's not working.

Marcus Buckingham and Peter Drucker have been real pioneers in the work of encouraging managers to use their energy to build strengths. When I'm in my weaknesses on the Red Platform I'm thinking,

"I hate this."

"Will this ever end?"

"This is going to take forever."

"Thank God this is nearly over."

When I'm working out of my strengths on the Green Platform I'm thinking,

"This is fun."

"I could do this forever."

"This is perfect for me. I just love this work."

When I'm working out of my weaknesses I'm feeling frustrated and I'm just into compliance. I'll do what I have to do, but I'm not engaged. I'm watching the clock. Time drags. Will five o'clock ever come?

When I'm living out of my strengths I'm in the zone, in the flow. Time passes and I'm not aware of it. I'm having fun. And that's the key. Find someone who can find fun in what you call work.

Steve Jobs had it exactly right when he declared: "The only way to do great work is to love the work you do."

Those who love what they do don't have to work a day in their lives. People who are able to bring passion and fun to their business and their families have a remarkable advantage, as passion and fun are contagious for their customers, colleagues and families

In another Gallup Study 80,000 successful managers were interviewed. They used up 120,000 hours of tape in researching what was the key to their success.

The answer was allowing people to become more and more of who they really were. To be yourself in a world that is doing its best to make you into somebody else is one of the toughest battles you'll ever fight. As Oscar Wilde put it: "Be yourself, because everyone else is already taken anyway."

Oprah Winfrey puts the importance of being yourself very well: "I had no idea that being your authentic self could make me as rich as I've become. If I had, I'd have done it a lot earlier."

In other words, by creating the space where people could become more and more who they really were, they helped ducks to be better ducks. They helped hens to become better hens.

These successful Green Platform managers had the ability to discover what was unique and great about an individual and they constructed the work, the job, and the role around that person's core strength. They helped people to really become more and more of who they really were. Successful Green Platform managers saw workers as individuals around whom they built jobs.

If we are to improve in life you have to ask yourself just two fundamental questions. The first one is: "What is your gift?"

And the second one is: "How are you going to use it in the service of humanity?"

By doing this there's a fair chance you won't end up as a hen with some silly manager teaching you to swim. Red Platform managers saw employees as workers who fulfil roles. These unsuccessful managers just took jobs and assigned those jobs willy-nilly to people at random.

Our hen is desperate to please because she has a mortgage and a young family to educate and jumps as he demands. She's desperate so she over-promises and under-delivers. She's not at her best with customers. You've given her the tools and training to do the job, but you complain that she still won't do it properly. She's continually stressed. So are you. The blaming and complaining goes on and on. It's pure Red Platform living and working.

Managers like that have no alignment with the gift of the person they are talking to, not an iota of an idea of their core strength or their best working role. They have Mozart milking cows and Michelangelo as a waiter in an Italian restaurant, but not within a mile of a block of marble, a hammer and a chisel or a tube of paint. And we talk about "flourishing" on the Green Platform. It's hard for a round peg to flourish in a square hole.

On the Green Platform you discover your strengths and you

play to your strengths. Then your weakness is someone else's strength. Together you can build a complementary team and you can unleash all sorts of hidden creativity and potential. Customers and colleagues will notice a massive difference when you and your team are working and living on the Green Platform from your natural core strengths, gifts and talents. Everyone wins.

Now while working out of your strengths and achieving and even exceeding your Fiercely Important Goals is important, even more important is who you become in the process. What kind of person do you become in the process of achieving your goals? A happier person on the Green Platform or a more miserable goal achiever on the Red Platform?

CHAPTER 23

GOAL
What Type Of Person Do You Become?

NOW that you have identified your three Green Platform Fiercely Important Goals (FIGs) and you have started down the road towards achieving them, there's a further question to keep in mind as you travel that road.

What kind of a person do you become in the process of achieving all your Green Platform Goals? Are you a happier, healthier, more creative, more joyful person in the process of achieving your goals, or are you a tired, cranky, miserable, black-eyed, burnt-out Goal achiever.

Sometimes people have a clear FIG: "To increase sales by 20 per cent in the next quarter." And they achieve it and maybe exceed it. But there is so much blood on the floor which has ended up turning your Green Platform FIG into Red Platform one.

How do you avoid this? You should set a big enough Goal so that in the process of achieving it, you become a greater person by far than you ever dreamed possible. That way, you'll have a pure Green Platform Fiercely Important Goal.

In the absence of clearly defined goals, things that matter least take over from things that matter most. Sometimes we can do very well what we should not be doing at all.

There is a formula I use to keep this achieving/becoming balance. It's called writing VERY SMART Green Platform Goals, ones that can give us a very clear visualisation of what we want to achieve and energises us to become more than we've ever dreamed of being in the process of achieving the goal.

Very smart Green Platform Goals are Visualised, Energising, Rewarding, Yearly, Specific, Measured, Agreed, Realistic and

Time-bound. Let's take a further look at the qualities of great FIGs.

V-isualised: See the FIG already achieved. Hear it. Feel the warmth of the words.

E-nergising: The goal must be something you are passionate about. It must have meaning and purpose. At best it will make the world a better place and it will contribute to humanity. It is underpinned by a powerful "Why?"

R-ewarding: When you write down your goal, write out the reward you will give yourself and others in your celebration of achieving your goal.

Y-early: Have three major goals for each year. Three FIGs – Fiercely Important Goals. Then chunk each one down into bite-sized chunks. Specific tasks to do each day to achieve your FIG.

S-pecific: Make sure your goal is focused and specific, not a vague, abstract generality.

M-easurable: What gets measured gets done. The journey of a thousand miles starts with a single step. The first step. Martin Luther King Jr. talked about "Taking the first step in faith." You don't have to see the whole staircase. Just the first step. And it doesn't matter where you are coming from. It only matters where you are going.

Take that first step. Life rewards DAN. Decisive Action Now. Life doesn't reward HAL. Hesitant Action Later. Do not wait; the time will never be "just right." Get it going and then like a heat-seeking missile you'll self-correct to your goal target.

A-greed: Your goal must be holistic and agreed with your key stakeholders. Make sure you have total 'buy-in,' from the people involved in accomplishing your goal. Those who have accomplished great goals in their lives have always paid tribute to the support they got from their background team, their family and their friends.

R-ealistic: But stretching. The greatest enemy of the human potential again is the comfort zone. Stretch goals get us into our excellence zone. We should do something every day that stretches us, gets us out of the 'same old, same old' always doing what we've always done rut. The only difference between a rut and a grave is depth.

T-imebound: A goal without a deadline is a wish or a fantasy, and that's a goal without energy. Did you ever notice how focused we get on revision three days before an exam.

Provided we get some oxygen in our heads from exercise, and a normal amount of sleep, we have enormous amounts of energy. We don't run out of energy ... we run out of clear goals with powerful "Whys" and deadlines.

Have you ever been lounging around on a Saturday morning, relaxing, taking it easy reading the newspaper. Then you get a phone call. Visitors are coming and they'll be there at 12 noon. Do you suddenly get energy? Are you up and about cleaning the place and getting in some nice food for lunch. It's the same energy you had earlier, but with a fresh and powerful "Why" and a deadline. They are on their way.

Once you get started, once you get going, you'll get momentum and not only will the Universe get out of your way, but it will conspire with you to make all your FIGs and dreams come true.

We have heard for years now that the key to goal achieving is smart work, not hard work. To work smartly, we need to discover the 20 per cent of tasks that deliver 80 per cent of our results. It's time to discover these vital few things, our 20 per cent and focus like a laser beam on those tasks leaving behind the swamp of the trivial many that keep us bogged down in our 80.

CHAPTER 24

GOAL
Get Things That Matter Most Into Your Jar

WHEN you ask CEOs what they look for in people they promote to senior management, inevitably they come up with two qualities:

1. An ability to prioritise, and

2. A sense of urgency.

Once we understand what's called the Pareto Principle, it's easy enough to prioritise. The Italian economist's principle states that 20 per cent of our tasks deliver 80 per cent of our results. In the world of business you need to get rid of your 50/50 mindset. Growing up on a farm in Co. Cavan we operated the 50/50 mindset. If we were sweeping the yard, my father would always say, "Take it out of a face."

"A face," was his saying. He meant, "Bring it all with you. Not just 20 per cent in the middle of the yard. No, the whole yard, beginning at one wall and working across to the other wall."

From the time Pareto discovered that 20 per cent of people controlled 80 per cent of the wealth, people started to focus on the other 20 percent. They use the Pareto principle in all different sorts of areas – the idea that by doing 20 per cent of work, you'll deliver 80 per cent of the results. They were astonished to discover the 20 per cent of tasks actually do deliver 80 per cent of results.

Or in terms of quality improvement, a large majority of problems (80 per cent) are produced by a few key causes (20 per cent).

In general we can say that:

◆ 20 per cent of thieves account for 80 per cent of the value of all crime.

◆ 20 per cent of drinkers consume 80 per cent of the beer.

◆ 20 per cent of any community's population utilises 80 per cent of its resources.

If we look at our own personal lives, we'll find that about:

◆ 20 per cent of the time we spend at work accounts for 80 per cent of what we achieve.

◆ 20 per cent of our clothes are worn 80 per cent of the time.

◆ 20 per cent of the carpets in our homes get 80 per cent of the wear.

◆ 20 per cent of a menu we choose 80 per cent of the time.

So if you have a list of 10 things to do, two of the things on that list are more important than the other eight in terms of results.

In fact, often one of those tasks can be worth more that the other nine. In terms of The Green Platform Goal Achievement process, it is essential to drill down and find out what are the 20 per cent of your tasks that deliver 80 per cent of your results.

Now get out a sheet of paper. Write down everything you did for the past three weeks. Then draw a line down the centre of the page and put down two headings – a 20 per cent column heading and an 80 per cent column.

Under the 20 per cent heading write down the 20 per cent of your tasks that delivered 80 per cent of your results. Then focus single-mindedly on this 20 per cent.

Sometimes managers say to me: "Yes, but a few of those things down in the 80 per cent are very important too."

Well, if they are that important, why aren't they up in the 20 per cent? You are going to do things in order, one thing after another, one 15 minutes after another, hour after hour throughout the day. Why not do the most important things first? Things that matter most should never be at the mercy of things that matter least.

A good way to find out how you should prioritise is to ask yourself, "What are the consequences of doing this now or not doing this now?"

Consequences are the key to prioritisation.

When you proactively get on the Green Platform, you lock on

like a laser beam to your 20 per cent, that vital 20 per cent of your activities that deliver 80 per cent of your results.

After a few weeks where you are totally focused on your 20 per cent and locking on to them until this process becomes a habit, then focus on your even more vital 4 per cent – that 20 per cent of your 20 per cent that deliver 96 per cent of your results.

Then you are ready for your Green Platform Bullseye. That's the 20 per cent of your 4 per cent, your 0.8 per cent.

Now with your Green Platform Bullseye you are doing what only you can do in the most efficient and effective manner possible. You are firmly on the Green Platform. You are doing what you love and loving what you are doing. You're in the zone. As an owner/manager you are not just working down in the woods in the company, you are up at 30,000 feet working on the company. Negotiating that deal that will make all the difference. You're working smarter, not harder.

But when you are in your 80 per cent you are back as the busy fool or the headless chicken reacting on the Red Platform. Your life is consumed with activities rather than results. You are working long hours. You haven't time to exercise. You're eating on the run where fast food is mere fuel, but never ever a celebration. You are working harder at what doesn't really work. But you're on the Red Platform and you're too busy to stop. You're having a nervous breakdown, but in instalments. You have no idea that there is a different platform, and a whole different way of living. You can't even catch sight of the Green Platform. You are on your Red Platform horse galloping off in the wrong direction but in too much of a hurry to stop and ask for directions. You are a person loaded with worry and in a terrible hurry.

MONTHLY ROCKS IN THE JAR

One way to get people into their 20 per cent is to get them to write out a major Monthly Rock Goal. Why call a monthly goal a Rock?

Your Monthly Rock Goal is your one big goal, your quantum leap goal for the month. It's the one thing that will guarantee you that you get on the Green Platform dealing with the vital few things that deliver real results and away from the trivial many things on the Red Platform that really don't matter in the long run.

What is the one big goal for the month?

The one that will be the difference that will make the difference. I got the idea of a Monthly Rock Goal to catapult busy people onto the Green Platform where they'll hopefully work smarter in their 20 per cent but not harder in their 80 per cent from the following story. I've heard many different versions of it, but this is the one I like.

One day, an old professor of the School of Public Management in France, was invited to lecture on the topic of – "Efficient Time Management" – in front of a group of 15 executive managers representing the largest, most successful companies in America.

The lecture was one in a series of five lectures conducted in one day and the old professor was given one hour to make his presentation.

Standing in front of this group of elite managers, who were willing to write down every word that would come out of the famous professor's mouth, the professor slowly met eyes with each manager, one by one, and finally said: "We are going to conduct an experiment".

From under the table that stood between the professor and the listeners, the professor pulled out a big glass jar. Then he pulled out from under the table a bag of stones, each the size of a tennis ball and placed the stones one by one in the jar. He did so until there was no room to add another stone in the jar.

Lifting his gaze to the managers, the professor asked: "Is the jar full?" The managers replied: "Yes". The professor paused for a moment, and replied: "Really?" Once again, he reached under the table and pulled out a bag full of pebbles.

Carefully, the professor poured the pebbles in and slightly rattled the jar, allowing the pebbles to slip through the larger stones, until they settled at the bottom. Again, he lifted his gaze to his audience and asked: "Is the jar full?" At this point, the managers began to understand his intentions.

One replied: "Apparently not."

"Correct," replied the old professor, now pulling out a bag of fine sand like flour from under the table. Cautiously, the professor poured the sand into the jar. The sand filled up the spaces between the stones and the pebbles. Yet again, the professor asked: "Is the jar full?"

Without hesitation, the entire group of students replied in unison: "No."

"Correct," replied the professor.

And as was expected by the students, the professor reached for the pitcher of water that was on the table, and poured water in the jar until it was absolutely full. The professor now lifted his gaze once again and asked: "What great truth can we surmise from this experiment?"

With his thoughts on the lecture topic, one manager quickly replied: "We learn that as full as our schedules may appear, if we only increase our effort, it is always possible to add more meetings and tasks to our days."

"No," replied the professor.

"The great truth that we can conclude from this experiment is: If we don't put all the larger stones in the jar first, we will never be able to fit all of them in later. In fact if we put in all the trivial gravel and sand first we won't be able to put in even one large stone." The auditorium fell silent, as every manager processed the significance of the professor's words in their entirety.

The old professor continued: "What are the large stones in your life? Health? Family? Friends? Your Major Goals? Doing what you love? Fighting for a Cause? Taking time for yourself?

"What we must remember is that it is most important to include the larger stones in our lives, because if we don't do so, we are likely to miss out on life altogether.

For each month, we should have a major Monthly Rock in the

Jar. So what are your big Rocks in the Jar for the next three months? That's the first column in the chart below. What is the major obstacle to those three Rocks? What's keeping you on the Red Platform? What are the Rocks on the Road? What's stopping you? What are the stumbling blocks. That's the second column below. How are your going to remove those obstacles and turn your stumbling blocks into stepping-stones? How are you going to bulldoze those Rocks off the road? That's the third column below.

Month	Rock In Jar	Rock On Road	Rock Removal
	Major Goal	**Obstacle**	**Bulldozer**
Month 1	Rock 1	X	✔
Month 2	Rock 2	X	✔
Month 3	Rock 3	X	✔

Then you push the idea to another level and you ask yourself: 'What are the Large Stones in my Life?' And once you identify them, be sure to put them first in your 'Jar of Life' or your 'Wheel of Life'.

So if you imagine your life to be a wheel, and within the wheel you have eight segments divided by spokes. Let's call the first segment 'work,' and the next one, 'physical exercise/health' and the next one 'partner/family,' then 'personal development,' 'finance,' 'spirituality,' 'social/fun time,' and finally 'contribution.'

If you were to fill in each one on a scale of 1 to 10 with 1 at the centre and 10 at the circumference ... how would you rate each segment? Is work nine and physical exercise two?

What we're looking for here is work/life balance. Most of us end up initially with a very wobbly wheel with "work" taking up the most time. Would it be possible to get more balance around the segments and a more circular wheel?

Usually we get one very wobbly first wheel where work is away out of proportion, near 10. Aim to push every section out to six or seven in the next six months. By activating the Green Platform 20 per cent at work you can double your productivity, halve your time and get work back to its proper place in your life. No one on his or her deathbed ever said: "I wish I'd spent more time at the office."

BALANCING THE WHEEL OF LIFE

Here's a helicopter view of current reality in my life to help me discover the gaps and balance to be achieved in My Personal Achievement Plan.

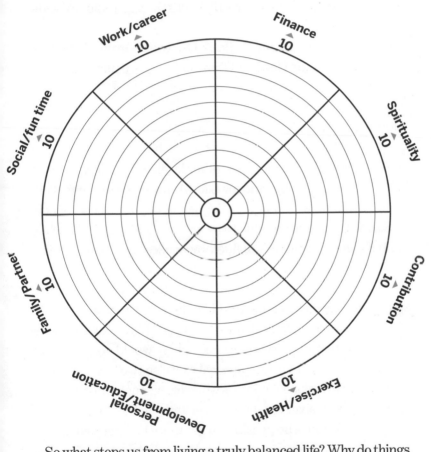

So what stops us from living a truly balanced life? Why do things that matter least get in the way of things that matter most? The real reason is to be found, not in a physical place, but in a psychological space – our Comfort Zone, the greatest enemy of our human potential. Is there a way to break free?

CHAPTER 25

GOAL
Escaping From Your Comfort Zone

OUR Comfort Zone is the greatest enemy of our goal achieving, the greatest enemy stopping us achieving peak performance. Our Comfort Zone is firmly planted on the Red Platform, the home of the whinging, whining, blaming victim.

So in general why won't we get out and do what we say we'll do when we should do it whether we like it or not? Why don't we just write down our goals and implement them? One reason is because it's a pain to move out of our goal-sabotaging Red Platform Comfort Zone. The Comfort Zone isn't a physical place; it's a place in our life that puts us on the Red Platform and tries to avoid anything that might be painful to us.

Strange as it might seem, merely escaping pain is not enough for us. We insist that pain be replaced by pleasure. We have developed a culture of 'instant gratification,' with an endless array of internet surfing, alcohol consumption, lounging in front of the television eating the aptly named 'comfort food,' manic gambling and even a certain kind of shopping. This is the era of born to shop, Red Platform retail therapy.

This Red Platform world feels soothing because it is familiar to us, even if deep down we know it is selling us short in life. The longer we dally on the Comfort Zone sofa, the harder we find it to get up, to get moving and to achieve our goals.

By largely residing in the Red Platform Comfort Zone, we pay a very high price for it in terms of selling ourselves short on our dreams and goals. Life provides endless possibilities, but along with them comes pain. If we can't tolerate discipline and pain, we cannot become fully alive.

The Comfort Zone is supposed to keep your life safe, but what it does is keep your life small. And miserable. To take advantage of the endless possibilities that life provides, we have to venture outside our Comfort Zone, off that Red Platform. When we do that, the first thing we meet is a Red Mist of pain.

Some people drive through tremendous amounts of pain, from rejection and failure in order to learn and develop and grow. They also handle the small, tedious pain required for personal discipline, forcing themselves to do the things we all know we should do, but don't do.

They have something that gives them the inner strength to endure pain, a powerful 'why,' or a sense of purpose. What they do in the present, no matter how painful, has meaning in terms of what they want to achieve in the future. Anyone can master their fear of pain and turn pain into power, but first they have to desire pain, not in a masochistic way, but in a totally empowering way. There is a way to get off that soul-destroying Red Platform. You have to act totally counter-intuitively and move towards that Red Mist of pain, through the Red Mist of pain and then beyond the Red Mist of pain.

A great rugby player one time discovered the secret of mastering pain and turning pain into power. He would demand the ball and run straight at the nearest opponent. He wouldn't fake him or run towards the touchline, no matter how much it hurt. "When I get up I feel great," he said. "Fully alive. That's why I'm the best. The other players are afraid of pain. You can see it in their eyes." He wasn't the most talented, he wasn't the most skilful, he wasn't the fastest, but he just plunged straight through the Red Mist of pain. That was his secret. On the other side of that Red Mist of pain he found the magic.

This seems crazy for most of us who spend our lives avoiding pain. But if you go straight for the pain, straight through that Red Mist you develop superpowers. He had discovered the secret of mastering pain. He had reversed the normal human desire to avoid pain and instead he wanted pain. He desired it.

He plunged through it and the Red Mist parted. Not because he was masochistic but because he had discovered the process of dissolving and shrinking pain. When you move towards it pain diminishes. When you move away from pain it chases you like a monster.

So pick a situation you're avoiding. Some kind of emotional pain. Not necessarily physical pain similar to the rugby player's pain. A phone call you're putting off. A goal you want to achieve. A task that seems tedious.

Imagine the pain you'll feel. Focus on the pain itself. See it like a Red Mist. Now rather than thinking about it, go straight through it. Go for the jugular of the Red Mist of pain. Go right through the Red Mist. Take instant action. Go through it. Go beyond it. High achievers go through that Red Mist of pain over and over again during a single day because the rewards on the other side are enormous.

If you're down at the sea, you can tip-toe around the edge putting your foot in and out as you stay stuck in that small world of your Comfort Zone, or you can run right through the Red Mist of pain and plunge into the freezing cold sea. Meanwhile all the others at tip-toeing around the edges of the ocean where it's actually colder than being in the ocean.

On the other side you'll find magic. You'll land on the Green Platform full of endless possibilities. You'll find freedom. You've broken free from that toxic Comfort Zone that keeps your life small, miserable and mediocre. You've left the cage of the half-lived life.

Beware of thinking about the activity rather than going through the Red Mist and doing it.

If you start thinking, Comfort Zone procrastination will set in and you'll go:

"Why do I have to do it?"

"I can't do it."

"I'll do it later."

Then this kind of thinking will lock you deeper into avoidance on the wrong side of the Red Mist in your Comfort Zone, jailed on the Red Platform.

Just do it now. Plunge through that Red Mist now. Beyond it is a new and a great and a wonderful world on the Green Platform.

I remember one time I was in Des Moines, Iowa in the United States. I had a long day's training workshop with managers and salespeople that involved being up at 5.00 a.m. Then, after the workshop I had a few hours drive to the airport hotel. I went up to my room on the seventh floor and lay down on the bed. I hadn't taken any exercise that day. I knew there was a swimming pool on the ground floor. My head was crying out for oxygen.

I thought: "I should go down and have a swim." But between the bed and the room door I could see that Red Mist of pain labelled 'avoidance.' Lying in bed, mentally but not physically tired, I was in my Red Platform Comfort Zone.

Then I said to myself: "don't think or rationalise, just do it."

So I jumped off the bed, put on the swimming togs, grabbed a bathrobe and headed down through the Red Mist. I did 20 lengths of the pool. When I came back up to the room I felt fantastic. But I almost didn't do it. I almost avoided the Red Mist. I almost caved in to ordinary human Red Platform sloth locked in my Comfort Zone.

To stop the "thinking and procrastination" bit you could have a few automatic motivational mantras or Green Platform PowerTalk to get you through the Red Mist.

"Bring it on."

"I love the great feeling through and beyond the Red Mist."

"The road through the Red Mist of pain sets me free."

Then go through it. When you run away from the Red Mist of pain it will chase you like a monster. But when you face it, go towards it and plunge through it and go beyond it, the pain disappears.

The majority of people will withdraw to their Red Platform Comfort Zone when what they try doesn't work. Only that small percentage will continually stretch, learn, grow and improve themselves. They will continually push themselves out into and through the Red Mist into their Green Platform Excellence Zone, and these are always the highest performers in every field.

There are two pains associated with any plan to achieve your goals. One is the pain of discipline, of doing it and the other is the pain of not doing it, regret.

The pain of regret is always the toughest pain. As Mark Twain said: "Twenty years from now you will be more disappointed by the things you didn't do than by the ones you did."

Success comes from the discipline that gets you through those Red Mists over and over again and firmly on to the Green Platform where exhilaration replaces pain. There are 46,000 steps and many Red Mists in a marathon, but the last five are the ones where the real magic kicks in.

The other side of pain.

Through and beyond those multiple Red Mists. That's where you find a new and a great and a wonderful world. You're firmly planted on the Green Platform. You've achieved your goal. Your arms are in the air. You're on cloud nine! You are screaming at the sky with joy. You've escaped the Red Platform cage of your Comfort Zone. You've escaped the greatest enemy that prevents you achieving your full human potential on the Green Platform. Mark Twain understood all about bursting through the Red Mist of pain when he said:

"So throw off the bowlines.
Sail away from the safe harbour.
Catch the trade winds in your sails.
Explore! Dream! Discover!"

The best way to break free from that cage of your Comfort Zone and through the Red Mist of pain is to make lists of the clear, inspiring goals that you want to achieve in life. Think it and ink it and you are on your way.

CHAPTER 26

GOAL
The Power Of Writing Lists

WE all have our own way of doing things but there are a number of old reliable ways that are particularly appropriate when it comes to making your FIGs work. On the Green Platform people who think it, ink it; they write it down.

Red Platform people don't bother with lists. They react at random. Research has shown that when people work from a list they are much more productive and efficient than people who just work at random.

Make A List: First you have your Three Green Platform FIGs,. Then your Monthly Rock Goals. From now on, make a decision to always work from a think it-ink it written list. Everything on your list should get you nearer your FIGs or your Rock Goals.

When something new comes up, add it to the list before you do it. You can increase your productivity and output by 25 per cent or more from the first day that you begin working consistently from a list.

Create Different Lists: You need different lists for different purposes. First, you should create a master list on which you write down everything you can think of that you want to do some time in the future, everything that will get your nearer your FIGs and Monthly Rocks. This is where you capture every idea that comes to you, or every new task or responsibility that comes up. You can then sort out and prioritise the items.

You Need A Monthly List: You should have a separate list for the month ahead. This may contain items transferred from your master list. Some of these monthly things-to-do should be helping you achieve your major monthly Rock Goal.

You should have a weekly list where you plan your entire week in advance. This is a list that is under construction as you go through the current week.

Top Five Daily Tasks: Then you transfer items from your monthly and weekly lists onto your daily list. These are the specific Top Five Daily Tasks that you are going to accomplish that day. This is where a small new discipline is required. Every evening write out those five most important things you have to do the following day, prioritise them and than begin with the first one.

Do it, this first one. Before emails, before anything else. Focus totally and single-mindedly on your first task.

Then the second one.

Then the third, fourth and fifth.

Do the hardest, the toughest one first thing in the morning.

Otherwise you'll have two pressures weighing down on you. The thought of doing it, and then actually doing it. Once you get used to this discipline of prioritising what you need for your goals as a habit, you will experience a feel-good factor which set you up for the day.

Make out your day's master list of the Top Five Daily Tasks the night before. Move everything from your previous list that you have not yet accomplished onto the next day's Top Five list if tasks are still a top priority.

The benefit of making out your list the evening or the night before is that it gives your subconscious mind the time to work on it all night long during sleep.

Often when you wake up, you will find a number of great ideas and insights swirling around inside your head as a result of putting the list together before going to bed.

To repeat, do these Five Daily Tasks first and foremost. Prioritise them and tick off the tasks on your list as you complete them. This activity gives you a visual picture of accomplishment. It generates a feeling of success and forward motion.

Seeing yourself working progressively through your list

motivates and energises you. Steady, visible progress propels you forward and helps you to overcome procrastination.

There are many versions of this story going around the corporate world, but here's one of them. Whether it's fact or fiction I don't know, all I know it that it works in real life.

Many years ago a man approached JP Morgan, held up an envelope, and said: "Sir, in my hand I hold a guaranteed formula for success, which I will gladly sell you for $25,000."

"Sir," JP Morgan replied, "I do not know what is in the envelope, however if you show me, and I like it, I give you my word as a gentleman that I will pay you what you ask."

The man agreed to the terms, and handed over the envelope. JP Morgan opened it and extracted a single sheet of paper. He gave it one look, a mere glance, and then handed the piece of paper back to the gent.

And paid him the agreed $25,000. Here's what was written on that the sheet of paper.

1. Every evening, write a list of the things that need to be done the following day and prioritise them in order of importance in terms of the results that you must deliver.

2. Do them in that order. As we saw earlier, life definitely rewards DAN (Decisive Action Now), not HAL (Hesitant Action Later.)

As you work through your lists, you will feel more and more effective and powerful. You will feel yourself living life on the Green Platform. You will bring discipline and organisation to your life. You will feel more in control of your life. You will be naturally motivated to do even more. You will think better and more creatively and you will get more and better insights that enable you to do your work even faster. You feel more powerful and competent. You eventually become unstoppable.

You'll be crystal clear on what you're going to do more of, and less of, on what you're going to stop doing and what you are going to start doing. And all the time you are staying flexible and open to new opportunities, but you'll be able to say "no" to all those time wasting things.

To embed these Green Platform tools in a team I usually ask two Green Platform Partners to meet for 15 minutes every Friday. We saw already that when you have a Green Platform Partner who will hold you accountable for achieving your goals, both "being" and "doing" goals – then implementation zooms from 40 per cent to an astonishing 95 per cent. We call it The GPPP: "The Green Platform Partnership Programme."

Here's how it works and is has been delivering dramatic results in the companies and organisations over the years.

You have a set time to meet every Friday. Then you have a short reflection around five questions related to The Green Platform Partnership Programme. You reflect on how you got on last week and areas that you can improve on next week. Here are the Famous Five Green Platform questions:

1. "Was I on the Green Platform this week? Did I slip off it? How did I get back on it? Did I help someone else back on it?"

2. "Was I aware of and working out of my 20 per cent this week?"

3. "Was I working out of my strengths this week?"

4. "How are my Fiercely Important Goals (FIGs) implementation progressing? Did I consistently write out my Five Most Important Tasks every evening this week, prioritise them and implement them first thing the following morning?"

5. "What progress am I making on my monthly Rock Goal?"

From the feedback I've been getting over the years, this has been revolutionary in goal-achieving and keeping morale high in many companies and organisations.

Your Green Platform Partner should be someone you trust who has your best interests at heart, supporting your "doing" goals and your "being" goals. They should be able to congratulate you and challenge you to be better and do better in a very positive and constructive manner.

DELEGATION

If you find that you are running out of time and the people working with you are running out of work, then you need to up your levels of delegation. There are four levels of delegation and everyone has a peak performance potential. You have to know where they are coming from, and meet them there as a co-worker, supervisor or manager by:

◆ Close Directing
◆ Coaching – Training
◆ Supporting or
◆ Delegating

There is nothing so unequal as the equal treatment of unequals. We all move from unconscious incompetence to conscious incompetence to conscious competence and then on finally to unconscious competence. There is growth. There is practice. There is learning. We keep on doing things poorly until we learn to do them well.

1. UNCONSCIOUS INCOMPETENCE

At the level of unconscious incompetence I'm sitting in the back of the car and I'm not even aware of the fact that I cannot drive. I'm just having a chat.

2. CONSCIOUS INCOMPETENCE

At the level of conscious incompetence I'm driving. I have an instructor. I'm tearing the gears. I'm gripping the wheel with a death grip. I'm out of my comfort zone. I'm watching footpaths, and mirrors and cars in front and behind. Tough going.

3. CONSCIOUS COMPETENCE

At the level of conscious competence I'm driving very carefully. I'm consciously changing gears. Keeping away from the footpath. Looking in my mirrors. Fully alert.

4. UNCONSCIOUS COMPETENCE

But I'm not really driving a car until I get to the level of unconscious competence. I'm driving along. I'm having a chat. I'm not even aware of changing gears. I'm still doing everything, but with unconscious competence.

That's mastery. Delegation is similar. There are four stages:

1. DIRECTING - CLOSE MARKING

The manager gives specific instructions, and closely supervises task accomplishment. "Just tell me what to do, and I'll do it." Some managers delegate at this stage and then swear they'll never delegate again. "If I want it done properly, I'll do it myself is their mantra." By that, of course, they mean they'll do it their way. Then we come to the second stage, coaching or training.

2. COACHING - TRAINING

Here you explain decisions and ask for suggestions.

At this level, the manager continues to direct and closely supervise task accomplishment, but also

(a) Explains decisions
(b) Asks for suggestions
(c) Supports progress

3. SUPPORTING - SHARING DECISION MAKING

Here the manager facilitates and supports the team member's efforts towards task accomplishment, and shares responsibility for decision making with her/him.

4. DELEGATE - NOW ONLY NOW DO WE DELEGATE

Here the manager turns over decision-making and problem solving to a 'Peak Performer.' Delegation is only appropriate for people who are peak performers.

Delegate the 'What' ... not the 'How.' Don't take the creativity out of it. Explain the 'Why?' Show how the job is important, how it is has purpose and is meaningful and how it will contribute to the overall goal.

Delegate the interesting tasks as well as the uninteresting ones. With peak performers, delegate the power and authority as well as the responsibility, and remember that delegation is not abdication. You are still responsible for the result.

In this way you'll achieve your FIGs on the Green Platform, and you'll nail every Monthly Rock Goal ahead of time. You'll also be disciplined enough to do your Five Daily Tasks first each day. Nothing will get you on the Green Platform quicker than that great feeling of accomplishment when you are doing what only you can do best in the most effective and efficient manner.

You'll also be very quick to spot the symptoms of bad time management.

CHAPTER 27

Symptoms Of Bad Time Management

THEY say that stress is when what you have to do and the time to do it are at odds. You are in traffic. You have an appointment at 11.00 a.m. It's now 10.30. It will take you 40 minutes to get to your destination. The traffic starts to move, but at a snail's pace.

Now your bad stress starts to build up. You are now slip-sliding on to the Red Platform. Here are some of the symptoms of Red Platform Time Management or should we say Time Mismanagement:

1. Continually overloaded schedule. Frequently working evenings and weekends.

2. Unable to meet deadlines. Constant delays. Always trying to catch up.

3. Quick decisions – despite the risk they involve.

4. Lack of depth in tackling problems.

5. Spending more time on problems than solutions.

6. Problem solving and fire-fighting rather than exploiting opportunities.

7. Inability to say "No."

8. The feeling of not being in control of the situation, of losing sight of your objectives and priorities.

9. Being a perfectionist. Procrastination due to perfectionism.

10. Stress, burnout, chronic fatigue.

11. Little time for family, social life or leisure.

12. Living with the urgent – not recognising or prioritising the important. (Exercise is important, but it is not urgent.)

PRACTICAL GREEN PLATFORM
TIME MANAGEMENT QUESTIONS

1. Have I decided on my life goals or my one big vision for my life?

2. Have I decided on my short term goals for the next six months?

3. Have I written out my three Three Fiercely Important Goals?

4. Have I done anything concrete today to help my short-term goals? My monthly Rock Goals? My long-term goals?

5. Have I practical supportive processes and plans in place to reach my goals?

6. Have I a precise idea of what I want to accomplish next week?

7. Do I know which hours of the day I am at my most productive?

8. Do I do my most important tasks during those hours?

9. Do I evaluate my performance at work according to results obtained, rather than the sum of my activities?

10. Do I set my priorities according to importance rather than urgency?

11. Do I delegate tasks to my subordinates/colleagues?

12. Do I delegate interesting work as well as routine work?

13. When I delegate a task, do I consider the power and authority as well as the responsibility to do it?

14. Do I delegate the 'How' as well as the 'What?'

15. Have I taken measures from preventing useless documentation (publications, reports, junk mail, junk emails) from arriving on my desk or desktop?

16. Have I gone through my files to eliminate all useless information?

17. During meetings, can I clearly sum up a situation, underlining:
- The main points of the discussion?
- The decisions to be taken?
- The tasks to be accomplished?
- Who is to do them and within what time frame?
- Timed progress reports?

18. Do I use the telephone and face-to-face meetings effectively to solve problems using paperwork and emails only when it becomes absolutely necessary?

19. Do I put the time going to and from work to good use?

20. Outside of work hours, do I take measures to free my mind from work?

21. Do I make an effort to make important decisions more rapidly?

22. If there is a crisis at work, will I be ready for the next one by learning from the experience and applying the measures necessary to prevent it happening again?

23. Do I take as much care in setting up deadlines for myself as I do for others?

24. Do I allow time for planning my work?

25. Do I continually test for how effective, necessary, efficient and appropriate the work is that I do?

26. Have I been able to terminate certain working methods that I know to be inefficient?

27. When I'm travelling on business do I use my time efficiently by having everything I need in my laptop case?

28. Do I make full use of the present moment and the task at hand rather then regretting the failures of the past and worrying about the future?

29. Do I regularly update my agenda to detect holes in the way I use my time analysing the urgent/important balance?

30. Do I encourage myself to practise habits that will make me more efficient in the use of my time?

31. Do I apply the Pareto Principle when I am faced with a number of tasks, all of which have to be done? Do I know the 20 per cent of my tasks that deliver 80 per cent of my results?

32. Am I proactive, in charge of my own time? Do I determine how my time is used rather than having it dictated to me in a reactive manner by circumstance and others?

33. Do I use my right brain and visualisation in goal-setting, and combine it with my left-brain in managing the objectives to achieving my goal?

34. What are my weak points in terms of Time Management? What are my strong points?

35. Do I spend my time the way I want to?

36. Am I working consistently out of my strengths, doing what I love and loving what I do?

37. Do I regularly feel stress at work, even if there is no crisis?

38. Am I happy in my work? Is there meaning in my life?

39. Have I an exercise routine that's like clockwork each day at the same time?

40. Can I clear my desk of papers (or files on my computer desktop) and put them where they should go in less than five minutes?

41. Am I regularly interrupted in the middle of important jobs?

42. Do I eat in the office?

43. Do I do the easy-to-do jobs first rather than the important ones that will deliver results?

44. Do I make excuses and put off doing things that I must do but don't like doing?

45. Do I get away for long weekends?

46. Do I have enough time for my favourite pastime ... reading, going to the theatre or the cinema?

47. Do I feel I should be doing something to keep busy?

48. Am I dominating the situation with important work or is it dominating me with urgent work?

49. Am I focused like a laser beam on my Prioritised Top Five Daily Tasks?

50. Every week do I have my Green Platform meeting with my Green Platform Partner for 15 minutes over the phone or face-to-face?

51. Am I crystal clear on the Five Green Platform Partner meeting questions?

52. Am I keeping it simple and having fun?

This is another trump card we have in Time Management and Goal Achieving. It controls 96 per cent of the way we act and move and have our being in this world. It's our subconscious. The challenge is that most of the time it is quietly sabotaging all our efforts to achieve our goals. But can we get it to work with us rather than against us. This will make a massive difference in terms of our results.

CHAPTER 28

The Role Of Your Subconscious

WE'VE seen already that the single biggest challenge with goals is implementation and consistency in that implementation. So what's stopping us getting on the Green Platform and straight into consistent and persistent goal implementation?

Treating the symptoms is like having a cancerous tumour on your leg and putting band aids on it. It's no use. The tumour has to be surgically removed.

Treating symptoms is like having a very bad bend on a cliff road and every day a few cars skid into the sharp bend and tumble down into the valley below. Now we can get very busy carrying the injured to hospital, preparing for funerals and clearing away mangled cars every day. We can even get the local school involved raising funds to sponsor an ambulance. Someone at some stage must stop this 'busy fool, headless chicken' treatment of the symptoms and say: "Let's take that bend out of the road on the cliff and put in strong steel protective barriers on the cliff road." Now, we've stopped treating the symptoms. No more cars tumbling over the cliff. Now we're tackling the root cause. Now we're cleaning out that tumour at the root. No more band aids.

THE SUBCONSCIOUS AS THE ROOT CAUSE OF IMPLEMENTATION SABOTAGE

Our subconscious is the root cause that stops us achieving our goals. Eighty per cent of the time it is quietly but effectively working away sabotaging our goals. It's working against us. That's the bad news. The good news is that we can actually get our self-sabotaging subconscious onto the Green Platform where it will work to enable us to achieve our goals.

Lets look at our subconscious. Your brain has two minds;

your conscious mind and your subconscious mind. They have two totally different functions. Your conscious mind is where you make decisions and it also gives you the power to be aware and to appreciate things. It's your conscious mind that moves into the White Space and makes a choice. It's the thinking, logical part of your mind that is trying to make sense of things. But the problem with the conscious mind is that it only controls 4 per cent of how you live and act.

Your subconscious mind controls the other 96 per cent of your actions on a daily basis. It's your subconscious blueprint that's really running your life. This blueprint is conditioned over years and years and its main job is to keep you in your Comfort Zone and to keep things the way they are.

It will urge you to bounce back from that Red Mist of pain so that you can't break through to your Excellence Zone. It wants to stop and block change, growth or personal development in your life. Your conscious goal-setting process presents a huge threat to your subconscious blueprint. To make any headway with our goals, we have to seriously look at changing your subconscious blueprint.

So we set our goals with our conscious mind, but most of the time our subconscious mind is busy sabotaging those goals.

Why?

Quite unaware, we have trained it to be our silent enemy as it continues to sabotage implementation of new goals . We need to re-train it to be our helpful companion working with us on our goal-implementation journey.

How does it sabotage our goal implementation? Here's how. People decide in January with their conscious mind to join a gym to get fit. The conscious mind is on a fitness roll for about a week, and then the subconscious mind takes over and that's the end of the gym. For another year, anyway. It quietly and subversively kicks in the old Comfort Zone routines and habits.

So how do we align our conscious mind to work with us on our goal achieving journey? There are a number of ways, and Green Platform PowerTalk is one of them.

Basically, this is a single positive present-tense sentence where you see and express or affirm your goal in its already achieved state. Done. Dusted. Completed.

As we've seen earlier, to be really effective a goal must contain a verb, a measurement and a time-frame.

Let's say you weigh 180 lbs.

So your goal reads like this: "I want to lose (verb), five pounds (measure), before June 8 (date)."

Green Platform PowerTalk: "I am now really enjoying being fully alive at 175."

It's your goal stated in the present tense in its already achieved state. You've not got it. It's 'as if' you've got it.

Once you create the conflict, the disorder between the picture of your current reality and your future goal picture stated in the present tense, your subconscious goes to work to resolve the conflict – to get the pictures to match, to move to the brighter picture. Your subconscious will always move towards the brighter picture.

It's like when you go into a room that's a real mess and very untidy. Total disorder. Now you have an inner picture of the room all neat, organised and tidy. This new inner picture becomes the brighter picture for the subconscious.

The gap, the disorder, the conflict between the outside picture (current reality) and your new inner brighter picture of the tidy room gives you energy. Your subconscious wants to close the gap. You roll up your sleeves and get to work tidying and organising the room. Then, when the outer room is tidied, your pictures match. The outer picture matches your inner picture.

That's really how we get energy. Deep within the subconscious is the need to create and restore this kind of order. If I say: "I feel very nervous," then your subconscious sees that as disorder. It goes to work 24/7 to bring about order again. To get the pictures to match. Once it gets you nervous, it thinks: "Well, now we're back in order. Conflict solved. Disorder scuppered. Order restored. Nervousness delivered. A perfect picture match. Job done."

Green Platform PowerTalk does something similar. It gives you that same energy 24/7. Green Platform PowerTalk really is "what you see is what you get."

Yes, it's that simple.

The subconscious loves rhythm so anything that it can hook into will work like "fully alive at 175." That's why we remember rhymes like, "sticks and stones will break my bones but names will never hurt me."

Green Platform PowerTalk is a powerful tool for manifesting your desires and making your goals come true. That's because the subconscious mind can't differentiate between actual reality and your Green Platform PowerTalk.

This means your subconscious processes your PowerTalk as being real and goes about using its powerful creative ability, and that of the nervous system, to actualise or manifest your Green Platform PowerTalk goals.

If your goal is to run a 10 kilometre race and raise money for charity, you see yourself crossing the line, completing the race. You freeze-frame that picture in your mind.

You snap that mental picture, put it indelibly into your brain and it becomes a new Self-Image for you.

"I now feel great having completed the race in one hour and eight."

You can snap yourself half way through the race: "I am now having fun and really enjoying my run."

Green Platform PowerTalk a simple positive, present tense sentence of your goal as if it's already achieved. The mind cannot hold two pictures at the same time. You think of an elephant and then a white fluffy rabbit. One first and then the other. The powerful by-product of Green Platform PowerTalk is that you are quietly eliminating those 'Automatic Negative Thoughts,' (ANTs).

By repeating your Green Platform PowerTalk over and over, it gets embedded in the subconscious and eventually becomes your reality. Repetition is the mother of skill. It's like mental push-ups.

That is why you need to be careful what you think and believe, because that is exactly what you will get. If you are repeating Red Platform PoisonTalk, then that too will tend to manifest easily in your life. Keep the picture clear and avoid wishy-washy phrases or the use of phrases such as "I would like" or "I may improve."

Avoid the future tense and possibility, as your subconscious won't process them.

Future: "I will weigh 175 lbs." That slips off your subconscious. No challenge. No conflict or "gestalt" in the present moment, and that's the fuel it needs.

Possibility: "I can weigh 175 lbs." And your subconscious replies, "and so can anyone." It won't do possibility.

Present tense: "I am now really enjoying being fully alive at 175."

Now you have the conflict or the challenge in the present moment that your subconscious loves. You've not got it, it's 'as if,' and you've created the disorder or conflict and now your subconscious will work 24/7 to bring about order and bring this into reality.

Do the Muhammad Ali thing: "I am the greatest." Live it in the now, not in some distant 'might' or 'maybe' land months or years down the line.

Keep empowering yourself when you find that you are in a Goal Achievement mode. Watch and notice your self-talk. Doubts disempower you more than you realise. Once you hesitate and say: "I normally give up on these things after a few weeks," you are opening a window for the Ego to creep back into your life and fence you off again into your Comfort Zone.

If you ask: "What can I do now to improve this?" or "How can I add something significant to my daily run?" then you are on the right track as your Green Platform PowerQuestion give an added turbo-boost to your goal implementation.

Researchers say that this kind of PowerQuestion boost can be as much as 50 per cent in terms of outcomes and solutions. Make a game of it in as far as you can. Give yourself little challenges. Now you've engaged your subconscious with your Green Platform PowerQuestions.

Your "How can I ...?" or "What can I ...?" questioning process by its very form elicits answers, and within these answers are strategies for actually achieving the goal or carrying out the task.

How does this work? Let's look at a presentation that you have to make. Green Platform PowerTalk gets you to the first level of excellence. "I am now really enjoying making this presentation." That the first stage. Now you are banishing fear, doubt and negativity.

The you turbo-charge your preparation with Green Platform PowerQuestions.

"How can I make a great presentation?"

Now what happens? You might say, "I've really done my preparation and I have some great relevant examples to drive home my main points."

Then you might even give yourself some tactical advice: "Last time I spoke too quickly, this time I'll slow down. Last time I spoke too much to my PowerPoint aid, this time I'll maintain eye contact with the audience."

The added boost that Green Platform PowerQuestions give us is that they prompt us to summon resources and strategies to actually accomplish the task, to achieve the goal.

Intrinsic motivation, your own personal inner powerful reasons or 'whys' to achieve your goal are powerful motivators.

You are much more likely to be highly motivated if it comes from within you rather than coming from someone else.

This is the second great advantage of Green Platform PowerQuestions as the answers they elicit connect to your reasons for doing something and many of those reasons come from deep within your subconscious.

When you add Green Platform PowerQuestions to your Green Platform PowerTalk you have a powerful combination of tools to change and retrain your subconscious and tackle the root cause of goal implementation sabotage.

What's daily life like inside our subconscious?

On average we have 50,000 thoughts a day. In terms of achieving our true potential what's hugely important is to discover how many of those thoughts are negative?

It can be quite shocking to discover that 80 per cent or 40,000 of our daily thoughts are negative. We're so surrounded by negativity we're as unaware of it as fish are aware of the water in which they swim.

Negativity seems to be in the very air we breathe.

"It's not that easy."

"Too much paperwork."

"We tried it before and it didn't work."

"How could you be so stupid?

"Just when we thought we were getting somewhere along comes this."

"You'll be the death of me, you'll drive me to an early grave."

"That's a terrible day."

"This day is going from bad to worse."

"Nobody appreciates what I do."

"You could kill yourself working around here for all anybody cares."

Keep in mind always that your subconscious cannot separate a real experience from an imagined one.

Remember the formula: I + V = R. (I is Imagination + V is Vividness really means R which is Reality for your subconscious).

Let's look at the process again. We have a thought. We feed it into our subconscious that is our unquestioning slave (it cannot choose, it can only obey), and it will search the inner filing cabinet of our subconscious to find that file to match that thought.

Whether it's negative or positive doesn't matter a whit to our subconscious. Its obedience is total and unconditional.

If you feed in a negative thought such as: "I'm feeling miserable and pretty useless," your subconscious won't say: "Hold on a second, this thought is bad for you and it's going to weaken you and actually make you more miserable."

It won't act for your good, and it won't act for your bad, it will just obey. Every time. It is after all your totally obedient slave. "Yes, sir, no sir, three bags full sir."

If I make believe that I have achieved my goal with Green Platform PowerTalk, the subconscious is triggered to focus in on the brighter picture that I've just dreamed up.

Positive thoughts actually give you energy and strength while negative thought really weaken you.

GREEN PLATFORM POWERTALK EXERCISE

Here's a short kinesiology exercise you can do to observe this strengthening and weakening in action.

Get a partner. Get him or her to stretch out their arm parallel to the floor, straight out. Then with two fingers just put some pressure on their wrist and ask them to keep their arm locked straight out. Flat. Just a small bit of pressure. Ask them to resist your pressure.

Then remove your hand and lead them in negative thinking. You say the negative phrase and get them to say it after you. This is Red Platform PoisonTalk.

"I'm tired."

"I'm fed up."

"I feel miserable," and so on.

Now observe their arm. Normally it will have dropped somewhat. Then take your two fingers and put a little bit of pressure on their wrist and watch how easily their arm will bend down with your slight pressure towards the floor.

Get them to shake themselves out and back to the original

position with arm outstretched parallel to the floor. Impose a little pressure just to test the strength. Ask them to resist your pressure.

Then take the lead in positive thinking as you do in Green Platform PowerTalk.

"I am confident."

"I am positive."

"I am strong."

"I am fit."

"I feel great," and so on.

Then test their arm again. You'll find it probably will be raised slightly towards the ceiling and rock solid when you put pressure on it to move it down towards the floor.

Green Platform PowerTalk empowers and strengthens you while Red Platform PoisonTalk disempowers and weakens you.

VISUALISATION EXERCISE

You can do a similar exercise with visualisation. Having tested the energy in the arm, then get the person to visualise themselves coming out of a concentration camp starved to the bones, weak and exhausted. Ask them to imagine lifting a heavy dumbbell weight. You'll find the arm goes weak and you'll easily push it towards the floor.

Next, invite them to shake out again and now with arm extended, get them to imagine that they have just won the world bodybuilding championship. Encourage them to see themselves on the podium receiving the gold medal and let them hear the crowd roaring and applauding with delight.

Then test the arm. It will be rock solid.

You can do a similar exercise about truth and falsehood. As they hold out their arm, ask them their name, and get them to give you a false name. Their arm will automatically weaken.

Then ask them again, only this time get them to tell you their real name. You'll find their arm is strong again.

Your subconscious mind can only accept your PowerTalk as a

set of commands when you phrase them in the present tense, and make them positive and personal with lots of emotion.

The greatest enemy of the human potential on the Green Platform as we've seen elsewhere in this book is the "Comfort Zone." One way to stretch out of your comfort zone through that Red Mist of pain into your excellence zone is to bombard your subconscious with Green Platform PowerTalk, Green Platform PowerQuestions and new thoughts and images of your goals as if they are already complete. Winners do this all the time.

Winners do the kind of things that losers don't want to do. The hard things. The challenging things. They do it by enjoying the process, but at the same time being very conscious and focused on the reward and then detaching from the reward. PowerTalk gets you into that feeling of having achieved the reward.

What we think about, what we visualise is what we ultimately achieve. What the mind can conceive, and believe through Green Platform PowerTalk it really can achieve. What we think about expands and grows and manifests in reality, and we attract more of it into our lives.

Green Platform PowerTalk enables, supports and empowers you to manifest your goals into reality in a very focused and direct way.

Now, as always with your goals and your Green Platform PowerTalk, they must be realistic and stretching for you. If you say: "I now really enjoy doing micro-brain surgery on everyone in this room," your subconscious will shut down on you, because it's not realistic for you.

If you are 100 years old it is not realistic to think you will complete a marathon in less than two hours and 10 minutes. It is, however, realistic to use Green Platform PowerTalk to get yourself to complete a marathon at the age of 100. One man ran a marathon in Toronto when he was 100. It took him over eight hours to complete it but he did it. That's what you'd call a 'real stretch goal.'

Mostly you don't get what you want because you are creating your life unconsciously by default instead of consciously designing it. Life, as we saw earlier, is really responding to you, not merely happening to you.

CONFLICT & COUNTER-INTENTION

Too often conscious goal-setting thoughts and your unconscious programming are in conflict. We don't deliberately or consciously sabotage ourselves but through limited, mostly automatic unconscious beliefs, and negative, unexamined habitual patterns, we are creating our lives by default.

We cannot achieve success by simply slapping positive Green Platform PowerTalk on top of a lifetime of negative expectations and beliefs buried deep in our subconscious and reinforced by our automatic everyday default thinking on the Red Platform. We need to look deep into the subconscious and see the limiting beliefs and habitual self-sabotaging habits and stumbling blocks that are holding us back.

Green Platform PowerTalk is about deleting those negative beliefs that stands between you and what you want. Once you become 'conscious,' and notice what is happening in your life and why you don't have what you want, you are destined to live a life on the Green Platform that is free of fear, doubt and worry.

Now as we saw earlier with Genevieve dropping the eggs on the floor when I said: "Don't drop them," our subconscious doesn't process negatives. It won't process words like 'not,' 'don't,' 'instead of' or 'without.'

"Don't think of a white rabbit," and there's the white rabbit. Your subconscious will always zoom in on the picture, and the more emotion associated with the picture, the faster the zoom. Just like a heat-seeking missile it zones in on the picture and gets a turbo-boost from the depth of feeling connected with the picture. Pictures and emotions are grist in the mill of the subconscious, and it will always focus and put attention on the picture that is brightest and has the most powerful feeling attached.

It has an automatic delete button for 'not,' 'don't,' 'instead of' or 'without.' Say to a child, "Don't bang that door," and bang goes the door.

Deep within our subconscious the age-old law of attraction kicks in giving us more and more of what we focus on whether we like it or not and whether we know it or not. Here's some examples of Poison Talk creating a vibrational match magnetically attracting more of what you don't want:

I don't want to spill anything on this suit really means: I want to spill something on this suit, and to spill many more things on lots of other clothes.

I can't handle all this work really means: I want more work than I can handle from more and more people.

I don't want to argue with you really means: I want more and more arguing with more and more people.

Don't speak to me like that really means: I want you to speak to me like that over and over again and I want lots and lots of other people to speak to me like that as well.

I don't want to catch the 'flu really means: I want to catch the 'flu and a lot more things too.

Most people are continually giving themselves suggestions for bad feelings, inaction and lack of confidence, and then wonder why they feel so bad.

According to psychologists Albert Ellis and Aaron T. Beck, "Negative thoughts are not a symptom of depression. They cause depression." They reversed the old thinking that depression causes negative thoughts and discovered in their research that negative thoughts actually cause depression.

On the other hand if you are confident, positive and optimistic and using Green Platform PowerTalk you will attract more positive things into your life. Every thought on what you want in your life becomes a vibrational match magnetically attracting more of what you want. Here are some examples of Green Platform PowerTalk that will activate this vibrational match:

"I am confident, positive, strong and secure!"

"I can do it!"

"If it is to be, it is up to me!"

"Every day in every way I am getting better and better."

"I smile at obstacles and always see solutions."

"Because of my leadership I inspire people and bring the best out of them."

"I create the space where people can become more than they've ever been before, more than they've ever dreamed of being."

"I continually catch people doing things right."

"I shine a light on what is right."

"Every day in every way I am getting better and better."

The subconscious really needs focused direction. Green Platform PowerTalk gives your subconscious focus and clear directions and clear signposts to your goal and it is always focusing on what you actually want to attract and create in your life. You're giving your subconscious what it craves for: Direction and clear commands given with vivid highly visual emotionalised pictures.

Your challenge is always to get its obedient "Right away, Sir," or "Right away, Mam," working for you and not against you.

Without this clear direction your subconscious is like a boat drifting on a lake. With Green Platform PowerTalk you put an engine and a rudder on the boat and give it direction.

In short Green Platform PowerTalk is a series of thoughts that you repeat over and over until they become beliefs that in turn spurs the subconscious to act on them. Green Platform PowerTalk is a great tool when it comes to creating change.

The power is not only in its ability to create situations and circumstances enabling you to achieve your goals, but Green Platform PowerTalk also helps you eliminate negative thinking.

The subconscious is this powerful force that controls 96 per cent of our habits and behaviour. There are four images that will help you illustrate the subconscious and how it works in your life.

(a) The first is as an iceberg, with most of it submerged.

(b) The second is an unquestioning slave.

(c) Thirdly, the subconscious is like your inner miles-long filing cabinet.

(d) The last image of your subconscious is that of an elephant.

1. THE SUBCONSCIOUS AS AN ICEBERG

With the subconscious the chunk of the iceberg under the water is a massive 96 per cent. So the conscious logical goal setting part is that small pyramid above the water, a mere four per cent.

2. THE SUBCONSCIOUS AS YOUR UNQUESTIONING SLAVE

The conscious mind can choose. It can give directions and orders. The subconscious cannot. It must obey just like an unquestioning slave. The thoughts that the subconscious mind receives from the conscious mind become commands that are instantly followed up on by your inner obedient slave. The subconscious is like the Genie from Aladdin's lamp who says: "Your every wish is my command." Its obedience is total and unconditional.

3. THE SUBCONSCIOUS AS A FILING CABINET

The subconscious is like your inner miles-long filing cabinet. It contains all your memories, all your wisdom, and your intelligence. It processes millions of messages. It's the source of your creativity. It stores and runs all your programmes of automatic behaviour like tying your shoelaces, driving your car or brushing your teeth. The problem this poses for us is that most of those programmes are centuries old handed-down, well past their sell-by date programmes. Many of them do not serve us well any more.

We need to change, override, upgrade or even completely

discard our old outdated programmes. How do we build a subconscious programme? First we get an imprint. We do something for the first time. The first time we learned to drive a car. We tear the gears. We kick-start and stall. We may even drive up on the footpath. But with repetition we get skill. Gradually we get into a pattern.

We go through the four stages of competence that we already saw earlier, and eventually we get into unconscious competence. Now we can harness the awesome force of habit. We have trained our subconscious. We are driving and having a conversation with a fellow passenger.

First we make our patterns or our habits, and then our patterns or our habits make us. That's why Picasso said one time: "I'm always doing what I don't know how to do so that I learn how to do it." We keep doing things poorly until we learn how to do them properly.

When you have a thought like: "I feel very nervous," then your subconscious receives that like a command from an army general and it clicks into instant obedience. It will do an immediate Google-like search through those miles of your filing cabinet drawer and then it will come up with the file 'nervous.'

It will say: 'Yip, nervous, we do this nervous file a lot.' It then begins to raise the tone of your voice, works at getting your palms sweaty and your knees shaking.

If, however, we rip off the 'nervous' label and replace it with a more positive label like 'I feel very excited,' then your subconscious will deliver excitement too.

4. THE SUBCONSCIOUS AS AN ELEPHANT

The last image of the subconscious is that of an elephant. The conscious mind (the bit of the iceberg above the water) is like an ant on an elephant's head. The elephant is the subconscious, that part of the iceberg below the water.

So the ant sets goals and moves down the elephant's back

heading for the tail. But in the meantime, the elephant is walking steadily forward in the other direction. There is no way that the ant's intention matches the counter-intention of the elephant, the subconscious. There is a massive conflict and there is only going to be one winner every time – the elephant, your subconscious.

For instance, you want to get fit and healthy. Your conscious mind, the ant, decides to go to the gym. You start your workouts.

Then the counter-intentions of your elephant kicks in. "I'm useless. When I look at the others I feel bad. I'm overweight. I'm a failure. I'll never get the hang of this. They're all laughing at me. I can't do this."

Soon the powerful counter intentions of the elephant will go one way while the ant is desperately trying to move the other way down the elephant's back. You have now trained the elephant as a massive self-sabotage machine, and you wonder why your fitness goals are not happening. You wonder why you stopped going to the gym. The elephant has an incredible unseen level of control.

You might say with your conscious mind ant: "I'll stop smoking," but your subconscious mind elephant is working out of habit and hates change, so this 'stop smoking' idea won't even get past your Gatekeeper RAS. And if it does somehow sneak in past your Gatekeeper RAS, your subconscious elephant will smother it fairly fast as it hauls out its buried subconscious beliefs that are in fact the real stumbling blocks:

"I get very cranky when I don't smoke," or "I get stressed too easily if I don't have a smoke," or "I think too much of my family to stop smoking."

Your subconscious will justify your decision to continue smoking. So the challenge is to replace those subconscious stumbling blocks and beliefs with positive Green Platform PowerTalk and Green Platform PowerQuestions – then nothing will stand in your way stopping you achieving your goal.

In the same way you can change any other habit or pattern. You've now removed the roadblocks. The challenge is always to notice, spot and change those hidden beliefs and roadblocks buried deep within your subconscious. They are the ones really leading and guiding the elephant.

If the ant thinks: "I need to make more money to pay all these bills," but the elephant, the subconscious mind has a buried stumbling-block-belief that "money is the root of all evil," then the elephant will win every time and sabotage any hope a making more money.

People who have the hidden belief that money is the root of all evil (rather than the love of money in itself that manifests as greed being the root of all evil), then their subconscious mind will sabotage any moneymaking venture.

If you can get your subconscious mind to see money as an energy that can transform and help you and others to grow, develop and live a sustainable life with dignity, then money starts to flow your way.

Years ago when I was living in a slum in the Philippines as a Columban missionary priest I buried 65 children who had died from hunger and poverty-related diseases in the final 90 days I was there. When I came back to Ireland I set about raising huge amounts of money to set up feeding centres, pig projects, hen projects, co-operatives, Grameen Bank projects and sewing projects.

I certainly didn't see money as evil. I saw the lack of money as truly evil. Affluence comes from the Latin word to flow freely. Money like water has to flow. When it becomes stagnant, then like stagnant water it soon starts to stink.

The trick is to train the elephant and to align it and have it going in the same direction as the ant. In other words, we have to get the elephant going in the opposite direction.

Your subconscious, your elephant has some very heavy built-in agendas. It wants to keep things the way they are. It hates change. It wants to keep things the same. It resists change with all its might. It holds all the cards.

The conscious mind is logical. The subconscious mind is emotional and couldn't give two hoots about the conscious mind (the ant) with its logic and its goal-setting.

That's why the ant, the conscious mind will make all kinds of New Year resolutions, but the subconscious mind, the elephant will scupper most of them within one week. Ninety eight per cent of New Year Resolutions don't last that one week.

If our elephant subconscious is going to change and work with us and walk in our direction, then it's the job of the ant to convince the elephant that change is both possible and safe.

Are there other ways apart from Green Platform PowerTalk and Green Platform PowerQuestions to train the elephant to work with us and walk in our direction rather than have it sabotaging all our goals and dreams?

There are a few more, four steps altogether in this process of getting the elephant to turn around and work with us on the Green Platform and stop all the sabotage.

The four steps are:

1. Visualisation With Emotionalisation

2. Green Platform PowerTalk

3. Green Platform PowerQuestions and

4. Mental Movie Making.

STEP ONE: VISUALISATION WITH EMOTIONALISATION

Step one is to visualise what you want to see happening and manifesting in your life. With visualisation we see a clear picture of where we want to go. You see the destination in a clear crisp high definition picture. You name it and claim it. Then the elephant begins to move in the same direction as the ant, the conscious goal-setting mind. This step incorporates the positive aspect of "The you you see is the you you'll be."

You keep feeding your subconscious Green Platform pictures of you being the best that you can be or whatever you want. You have to see it to be it. Like the blindfolded archer, you cannot hit a target that you cannot see.

Your subconscious works best with a clear emotionalised picture of your goal of what you want because your subconscious is really a goal seeking mechanism.

See it. Hear it. Feel it. Really feel the feeling of having achieved your goal. Picture what you want in great detail. Use a Vision Board or any kind of picture. The elephant only processes the clear pictures and images you see with real emotion. We easily attach negative emotions to negative pictures. Putting in positive emotion is more challenging.

We've seen how the subconscious mind resists change. Let's look at the way we normally handle that with children. Let's say your child is going to school for the first day. What normally happens?

You bombard his little subconscious with all kinds of pictures and images of going to school. "Oh, you'll be a big boy or girl now. You'll have schoolbooks. You'll get homework. You'll have lots and lots of new friends. You'll have a special teacher just for your class. You'll have a new schoolbag for your new schoolbooks. You'll have a special school lunch."

The visualisation process is massive.

Then on Monday morning, you're going to take the child to school at 8.45am. But he's nowhere to be found at 8.00 am. The child's not upstairs. Not in the kitchen. Nor in the bathroom. Then you go out to the car and there's the child, sitting in the car with his new schoolbag.

"What are you doing out in the car at this hour of the morning?" "But I'm a big boy (or girl) now. I'm going to school today. Then you say, "No, come back in. We're not leaving until 8.45."

The child can't wait to go to school, because of all the visualisation and positive PowerTalk. Now his subconscious sees that change is both possible and safe and it works with the child.

Now, let's say we don't do any of that visualisation or positive Green Platform PowerTalk. Say nothing to the child. Put him or her in the car, and drop them at the school on Monday morning. "There your are. It's your first day at school. Have a nice day. Love you, bye bye."

Then, what's hanging on to the bumper of your car as you drive away from the school? The child. No way is the little subconscious going to allow that massive change into the child's life. Again, it holds all the cards. It will resist it with all its might.

We wouldn't dream of doing that with a child, but we do it with adults all the time. Visualisation is a powerful first step in getting our subconscious elephant's blueprint to match ours and align with our goal implementation. It's the first signpost for the elephant turnaround and actually take us where we really want to go.

STEP TWO: GREEN PLATFORM POWERTALK

You follow your visualisation up by bombarding your elephant subconscious with Green Platform PowerTalk so that you create a new blueprint eliminating all those buried beliefs and stumbling blocks. This affirms your new vision. Once the elephant turns and heads in the right direction you'll see an explosive increase in your goal implementation.

Reprogramming the elephant with Green Platform PowerTalk as we've already seen goes something like this:

"I am confident, positive, strong and fit."

"I am fast, flexible, agile and accurate."

"Every day in every way I am getting better and better."

STEP THREE: GREEN PLATFORM POWERQUESTIONS

A third step in training the elephant is to keep using Green Platform PowerQuestions such as:

"How can I turn this around and enjoy the process?" ("How can I turn this elephant around and enjoy the process?")

"How can I improve my coaching skills?

"What's the one thing that I can do to improve this situation?"

Your subconscious elephant again loves a conflict or a challenge. Once you launch the "How can I ...?" question at it, it will go into overdrive and work 24/7 to come up with an answer that will be a solution to your challenge.

Unfortunately it will work just as well with Red Platform PoisonQuestions. "What did I do to deserve this?" and in no time at all it will tell you and depress you. Topping up your Green Platform PowerTalk with Green Platform PowerQuestions is the fastest, most effective and efficient way to stop the elephant's goal implementation sabotage. Once you get your subconscious on your side, working with you, you'll be solidly in the fast lane of goal achieving.

STEP FOUR: MENTAL MOVIE-MAKING

Make a movie of your ideal solution. See yourself, hear yourself and feel yourself succeeding in your inner movie. This will spur your elephant to keep moving in that direction. Your subconscious will always move to your brighter picture or your brighter movie. Always focus on 'movies' of what you want to create and attract into your life, not on what you don't want to create and attract into your life.

Make vivid mental movies of your dreams and goals. And that subconscious elephant, once you get him on the Green Platform, will work with you to achieve and indeed exceed your goals. You've got alignment. You are now creating your life by design, not reacting by default. You are both heading in the same direction. The hidden sabotage has stopped.

Central to aligning your subconscious and your conscious mind to work together to achieve your goals is Green Platform PowerTalk. Next we will take a look at the 14-steps for creating effective Green Platform PowerTalk that will turbo-charge our subconscious to work with us and travel in the direction we really want to go?

Control your self-talk with Green Platform PowerTalk or your self-talk will control and programme you with Red Platform PoisonTalk.

Olympic gold medal-winning hurdler Sally Gunnell never heard of Green Platform PowerTalk, but she actually used it all the time. She had a massive belief in the power of the mind to influence performance.

Sally had a bad chest infection and cold before the world championships. She said: "I taught myself not to let any negative thoughts come in because that's what the mind wants to do all the time."

Interestingly enough, she didn't say: "It was natural for me growing up in my family not to have any negative thoughts." No, she put in the work and taught herself to get off the Red Platform and onto the Green Platform with positive thoughts. "I used to just stop myself and turn it around and say: 'I can do this. I've eaten well. I've done everything I can.' I fed myself loads of quality thoughts until, I guess, the brain took it all in."

Gunnell won the Olympic gold medal in 1992 and her next big event was the World championships in 1993. However, a week beforehand she got a bad dose of a cold. She didn't use the cold as an excuse. She went straight on the Green Platform:

"I was feeding myself good thoughts. I told myself, 'I'm feeling fantastic. I can do this. I'm in the best shape ever.' Every time a negative thought started I wouldn't let it finish in my mind. I would stop it and turn it around into something positive: 'I feel really good. I've eaten fantastically well.'"

Not only did she win the world title, but she also set a new world record in the process.

"I was in shock that I'd done it. I was freaked out to think that I'd actually talked myself into that – into winning."

When Tiger Woods was as young as 12 he was using Green Platform PowerTalk.

"My Strength is Great."

"I Focus And Play With All My Heart."

"My Self-Belief Is Total."

"I Fulfil My Resolutions Powerfully."

"My Will Moves Mountains."

Virtually all of the top performers in the sporting world use some form of Green Platform PowerTalk. In the next chapter, we will consider the qualities of good Green Platform PowerTalk.

CHAPTER 29

Creating Green Platform PowerTalk

THERE are 14 guidelines for creating Green Platform PowerTalk:

1. GREEN PLATFORM POWERTALK IS PERSONAL
- NOT FOR SOMEONE ELSE, ONLY FOR ME

Green Platform PowerTalk start with the words, "I am ..." Two of the most powerful words in the English language. The subconscious takes any sentence starting with "I am ..." and interprets it as a command – a directive to make it happen. It then clicks into obedience.

"I am now positive about the job I am doing."

"I am happy and grateful that my family is healthy."

"I am now really enjoying keeping our home neat, tidy and organised."

Green Platform PowerTalk celebrates achievement in the first person. "I am ..." (You can also use: "It's easy for me ... or "Because of my ...")

2. USE THE PRESENT TENSE

Describe what you want as if you already have it, as though it is already accomplished.

Right: "I am now really happy driving my new Toyota Avensis. ("Now" locks it into the present tense.)

Wrong: "I am going to (Future) get a new Toyota Avensis.

Using the present tense instead of the future tense to the subconscious creates the gap, the disorder or the conflict. Add the word "now." This helps to keep it in the present and gets you a free pass through your Gatekeeper RAS.

The present tense creates the conflict or the gestalt that in turn generates the energy.

3. GREEN PLATFORM POWERTALK IS ALWAYS POSITIVE

Focus on what you want, not what you don't want. Do not describe what you are trying to move away from or eliminate.

"I don't want to smoke anymore." You're still feeding in the image of smoke into your subconscious.

"I'm not as big a slob as I used to be."

As we now know, the subconscious won't hear your "don't," "not," "without," "instead of," or "no." It only takes in pictures and the emotion connected with the picture.

Right: "I am now really enjoying the thrill of flying."

Wrong: "I am no longer afraid of flying."

4. GREEN PLATFORM POWERTALK IS BRIEF, SHORT, SNAPPY AND RHYTHMIC

Think of Green Platform PowerTalk as an advertising slogan. Write it as if each word cost €1,000. Short, rhythmic and memorable.

"I am confident, positive, strong and fit."

"I am fast, flexible, agile and accurate."

"I am fuelling every moment with the best that's in my now."

5. GREEN PLATFORM POWERTALK IS EMOTIONALLY CHARGED TO INCLUDE THAT GREAT FEELING OF HAVING ALREADY ACHIEVED YOUR GOAL

Use emotional-feeling words and make the experience playful and fun-driven. That put us wholeheartedly into the experience. Include at least one feeling word as if you had already achieved your goal.

Right: "I am feeling agile and great at 178."

Wrong: "I am maintaining my weight at 178 pounds."

6. GREEN PLATFORM POWERTALK IS PRECISE, FOCUSED AND SPECIFIC

Create high definition mental pictures. A clear vivid picture creates enormous magnetic energy. An abstract fuzzy vague picture creates little energy.

Right: "I am now really enjoying driving my new blue Toyota Avensis saloon."

Wrong: "I am driving my new car."

7. GREEN PLATFORM POWERTALK IS REALISTIC BUT STRETCHING

"I am now really enjoying doing micro-brain surgery," is not great PowerTalk for a cattle dealer. It's not realistic. It's out of reach. The subconscious shuts down. "I am now really enjoying my run," is realistic but stretching if you are starting exercise.

8. GREEN PLATFORM POWERTALK NEEDS ACTION WORDS

Include an action word ending with "–ing." The action verb adds power to the effect by evoking an image of doing it right now.

Right: "I am now confidently expressing myself openly and honestly."

Wrong: "I express myself openly and honestly."

9. RELEASE YOUR POWERTALK LIKE A BALLOON - WITH OPEN HANDS

Trust. No teeth gritted with bulldog determination. No clenched fists. Did you ever try to remember a name? Relax, and the name pops up. Loading coal on to a truck in the outer world is about effort. In the inner world it's about a relaxed focus.

Don't be attached to the result. Concentrate on your performance and you'll achieve the result.

Make your Green Platform PowerTalk and confidently relax.

10. GREEN PLATFORM POWERTALK - NO COMPARISONS

We always compare to our disadvantage. It's okay to model someone's good behaviour but comparisons are odious.

You should not say – "as good as" or "better than." You are

unique. You have something to accomplish on this earth that no one else can.

Never "I now really enjoy being better than ..." Or "Being as good as ..."

11. BALANCED

We make Green Platform PowerTalk in all areas of our lives, work, family, recreation, physical exercise, social, financial, spiritual, personal development, and contribution. All the way around your Wheel of Life.

12. GREEN PLATFORM POWERTALK HELPS US TO HONOUR OUR COMMITMENT TO OURSELVES.

When we break our word to ourselves ... no one knows. Nonsense. The whole universe knows. It's a Red Platform thing.

13. ADD: "OR SOMETHING BETTER FOR THE HIGHEST GOOD OF ALL"

Sometimes our criteria for what we want come from our Ego or our own limited human experience. Sometimes there is someone or something better available for us.

"I am enjoying driving my new blue Toyota Avensis or something better." (A Lexus wouldn't be out of the question.)

14. REPETITION - MENTAL PUSH-UPS

Write your Green Platform PowerTalk on cards. Put them on a CD, iPod, iPad or iPhone, Android or Smartphone. And repeat them, like a drip on a stone ... imprint, imprint, and imprint. They are truly mental push-ups. Repetition is the mother and father of skill.

A SIMPLE WAY TO CREATE GREEN PLATFORM POWERTALK

1. Visualise your goal. See it as you would like it to be. Associate

– place yourself inside the picture – and see things through your eyes. If you want a car, see the world from inside the car. You are driving it.

2. Hear the sounds and what people are saying when you've achieved your goal.

3. Feel the feeling you'll have when you have achieved your goal.

4. Describe your experience in a brief statement, including what you are feeling.

OTHER WAYS TO USE GREEN PLATFORM POWERTALK

1. Put 3 x 5 cards with Green Platform PowerTalk in strategic places around your home.

2. Put pictures of what you want to achieve in your goals where you'll see them.

3. Repeat Green Platform PowerTalk during "wasted time," waiting in line, exercising (between repetitions) or driving.

4. Record your Green Platform PowerTalk and listen to them on your iPhone, or Smartphone.

5. You can repeat your Green Platform PowerTalk in the first person ("I am, or "Because of my …" or "It's easy for me …")

6. Or the second person (You are), or the third person (Shc/he is) it's all still personal. For you. Not for another person. You are still talking to yourself.

7. Put Green Platform PowerTalk on the screen saver of your computer.

SOME EXAMPLES OF GREEN PLATFORM POWERTALK

◆ I have a positive expectancy of success in all I do, and I see all setbacks as lessons and learning experiences

◆ I love demonstrating warmth and love to my family in ways that are meaningful to them

◆ I am an attentive listener, and I value what others have to say

◆ Continual improvement is a way of life for me. I am always looking for ways to grow both personally and professionally

◆ I am really good at creating productive harmony and happiness among the people I work with

◆ Because of my leadership I inspire my team to achieve better and higher goals

◆ I love being very creative

◆ I enjoy and get enormous benefit from saying my Green Platform PowerTalk at least twice a day

◆ I really enjoy the little rewards I give the team after completing challenging assignments

◆ I now easily distinguish my important goals from my urgent ones

◆ I'm delighted that I now easily do the tough top priority job first

◆ I now easily motivate people according to their peak performance levels within their personality type

◆ I now easily inspire confidence in people

◆ I can now easily show appreciation

◆ I make a point of personally thanking people for doing a good job

◆ I now really enjoy listening to people.

GREEN PLATFORM POWERTALK
TO INCREASE CONFIDENCE

◆ I really enjoy life's challenges and I love learning from everything that happens in my life

◆ I love living each day with passion and power

◆ I now feel strong, powerful, happy, excited and enthusiastic

◆ I now have tremendous confidence in my gifts, talents and abilities

◆ I now really enjoy choosing the Green Platform of peace, joy and happiness at every moment of my life

◆ I now really enjoy the deep feeling of respect I have for myself and every person I meet each day

◆ I now really enjoy seeing every task as an unprecedented opportunity to achieve excellence

◆ I now really enjoy the freedom of forgiving myself and others easily

◆ I now really enjoy being proactive …fully awake and aware of all choices I make

◆ I now really enjoy being confident, prepared and ready to respond with love to every challenge

◆ I now really enjoy knowing that I can always choose peace, joy and happiness by going inside and reconnecting and remembering.

VIBRANT HEALTH AND ENERGY
ON THE GREEN PLATFORM

◆ I wake up each morning feeling healthy

◆ I now enjoy consistently thinking healthy, positive thoughts

◆ I now enjoy the silence of the quiet times as I breath slowly and deeply

◆ I feel great pleasure and health from the strength of my physical body

◆ I eat and drink wholesome food and drinks

◆ I now enjoy starting the day with an abundance of energy

◆ I go to sleep each night full of gratitude for my day, my health and my energy

◆ I drink lots and lots of water.

GREEN PLATFORM POWERTALK
TO INSPIRE CONSISTENT ACTION

◆ Don't get it right, just get it going.

◆ If it is to be it is up to me.

◆ Every day in every way I'm getting better and better

◆ I really enjoy taking massive and consistent action to achieve my goals

◆ I enjoy being a "do-it-now" person as I make my time serve me

◆ I really enjoy great freedom and pleasure as I get into action each day

◆ I now really enjoy just getting it going

◆ I now really enjoy doing the five most important things each morning to achieve my written goals.

Focus on your Green Platform PowerTalk clearly, yet in a light and gentle way. Don't strive too hard or put excessive energy into them. That would hinder rather than help. Like learning to swim, learning to relax in the water is important. Gently correct negative self-talk. Assimilate the positive and like a good gardener make compost out of the negative, replacing it with the lessons you have learned along the way.

SOME MISCONCEPTIONS ABOUT GREEN PLATFORM POWERTALK

Let's clear up some misconceptions about Green Platform PowerTalk. You cannot use Green Platform PowerTalk to affect somebody else's behaviour – that is you use our method to get somebody else to do something.

For example you cannot create Green Platform PowerTalk to make someone behave a certain way or make someone love you. You cannot use it to get somebody to do something that they do not want to do. You cannot use Green Platform PowerTalk to control somebody else – otherwise ruthless leaders all over the world would have their cronies reciting Green Platform PowerTalk to get people to behave a certain way.

It's just not that simple. You cannot use Green Platform PowerTalk to change something that has already happened or fix something that is already broken. Green Platform PowerTalk work best when they are connected to:

◆ You and

◆ Your behaviour and

◆ Your goals.

Let's say you want to improve a relationship with somebody and you want him or her to understand you better or listen to you when you speak. You can't say Jim is now listening to me or Elizabeth understands me better.

Remember you can't change the way somebody behaves with Green Platform PowerTalk. If you've been doing this and not getting results, now you know why.

Instead – you should be focusing on yourself and your actions. In the above example you would say something like, "I'm now finding ways to help Jim understand me better."

"I'm now saying the right things to help Elizabeth listen to me."

"I'm finding ways to convince Jim to listen to me and I'm now convincing John to listen to me."

Two things have happened here – one is you've taken your Green Platform PowerTalk and sent the message to your subconscious mind so that you do the right things to improve the situation.

Next – you've also instructed your subconscious elephant mind to provide you with the corresponding action to help you obtain the outcome you want. What follows is that you start doing things to create the outcome you want.

This is very different than saying: "Jim is now listening to me." (Passive) This depends entirely on Jim.

In that case you are doing nothing and trying to get somebody else to do something while you keep taking the same actions – you'll never get the results you want.

You cannot change someone else. You can only change yourself. Green Platform PowerTalk should reflect what you can do and what actions you can take to create the outcome you want.

It should be short and simple – and reflect what you want to happen and what you can do to make that situation happen.

When you recite Green Platform PowerTalk in your head – you train your mind to stay positive, think positive and more importantly it stops you being negative. You also get used to saying it.

Track your results – see if there have been improvements in certain areas of your life for which you've been using Green Platform PowerTalk. Even small improvements are positive signs.

Do you need to believe the Green Platform PowerTalk?

No you don't. We're making Green Platform PowerTalk or Red Platform PoisonTalk all the time whether we believe it or not.

"I'm tired."

"I'm fed up."

"I feel miserable."

Your subconscious believes this Red Platform PoisonTalk.

Green Platform PowerTalk is a powerful tool that can help you create the life you want and deliver the results you want. But you have to use it properly and you have to continue working with it regularly – to the point where Green Platform PowerTalk become such a habit that you find yourself defaulting into it all of the time.

CHAPTER 30

Treasure Waiting On The Green Platform

SOMETIMES CEOs say to me: "All this Green Platform stuff is fine, but what's it got to do with the bottom line?"

My simple answer is: "Everything."

The cost of the Red Platform, what researchers call, 'negative attitudes and negative behaviours' cost the economy of the US a minimum of $350 billion over the course of a year. That figure didn't take into account the problem of these negative toxic 'Energy Vampires' didn't leave their desks and contaminate others – which of course they did.

For companies on the Green Platform, the sky's the limit.

Dr Martin Seligman from the University of Pennsylvania did a 29-year study on managers. Those who were successful were firmly locked on to the Green Platform where they focused on the future, on their goals, on how to achieve them and they specifically caught people doing things well. When they failed, they saw failure as just temporary, and went into a learning, next-time mode: "What can I learn from this to improve it next time?"

Those who were unsuccessful were firmly welded on to the Red Platform where they focused on what went wrong and who to blame as they continually found people at fault. When they failed at something, they assumed failure was permanent, and moreover that they themselves were, in fact, failures.

At every level, from performance to profitability to cutting costs and raising staff morale – the Green Platform is the consistent winner all the time, every single year.

Over the past decade we've all seen the power of the Red Platform to destroy families, companies, banks, governments, developers and even the church.

It's time for a change.

It's a time for a real deep personal and structural transformation that happens when people become aware of the Green Platform and step on to it.

We do have a choice about the next decade.

After a destructive Red Platform decade, it's time for a constructive Green Platform 10 years to look forward to.

Once you become aware of the power of the Green Platform to change your life, your family and your team for the better, you find a great tool in day to day living.

It allows you to observe your negative thoughts. Then gently and compassionately change them. But don't make your mind a battlefield between the negative and the positive. Just simply step back on the Green Platform.

The process of simply stepping on to the Green Platform is beautifully illustrated in the following story where an old Cherokee chief was teaching his grandson about life.

"A fight is going on inside me," he told the young boy, "a terrible fight between two wolves.

One is evil, full of anger, sorrow, regret, greed, self-pity and false pride. The other is good, full of joy, peace, love, humility, kindness and faith."

"This same fight is going on inside of you, my boy ... and inside of every other person on this earth."

The grandson ponders this for a moment and then asks, "Granddad, which wolf will win?"

The old man smiled and said simply: "The one you feed!"

It's up to us which wolf will we feed every day.

Lao Tzu really understood the message in this wolf story and knew the difference between sabotaging your dreams on the Red Platform or achieving your dreams on the Green Platform when he said:

"Be careful what you water your dreams with. Water them with worry and fear and you will produce weeds that choke the life from your dream.

"Water them with optimism and solutions and you will cultivate success. Always be on the lookout for ways to turn a problem into an opportunity for success. Always be on the lookout for ways to nurture your dream."

Always be looking out for ways to nurture your dream with optimism, focus on solutions and feed your Green Platform wolf of "joy, peace, love, humility, kindness and faith."

We all dream dreams. That's where greatness begins as your inner dream begins to work its way outwards. First the dream, and then the reality as you take massive and consistent smart action to make your dream come true. Happy are those who are inspired every step of the way on their journey to their dream reading the signs and omens as they take inspired action along the way rather than bulldog-like forcing or shoehorning action that bulldozes life into their own mental linear cookie-cutter goals.

The bottom line is really that you don't set your goals to achieve your dreams; you simply download then. Your dream, your goals and your personal blueprint for magnificence are all already there inside you like an email on your computer.

But to live the dream, we have to first of all get on the Green Platform and wake up. Most of us don't wake up. We sleepwalk through life and dabble at things throughout our lives with little or no focus as we amble along on the Red Platform hauling our mental duvets to work.

Getting on the Green Platform and waking up to our own inner greatness is a powerful and transforming thing. It's a choice. And we do have the power to choose, to actually wake up. We are not our conditioning. We are not our stories.

Some people, however, never wake up, like the eagle in this story who lived his life trapped by his conditioning and stories sleepwalking through life on the Red Platform.

Once upon a time, a farmer found an eagle's egg away up in the cliffs, took it back to the farmyard and carefully put it in a hen's nest under a clucking hen.

The eaglet hatched with the brood of chickens and grew up with them. All his life the eagle did what the farmyard chickens did, and grew up thinking he was a farmyard hen.

He scratched the earth for worms and insects. He clucked and cackled. And he would thrash his wings and fly a few feet into the air.

Years passed and the eagle grew very old. One day he saw a magnificent bird above him in the blue cloudless sky.

It glided in graceful majesty among the powerful wind currents, with scarcely a beat of its strong golden wings.

The old eagle looked up in awe.

"Who's that?" he asked.

"That's the eagle, the king of the birds," said his hen-neighbour.

"He belongs to the sky. We belong to the earth – we're hens." So the eagle lived and died a hen, for that's what he thought he was. A case of the you you see being the you you'll be."

The eagle didn't wake up to his own greatness on the Green Platform. He never actually found his treasure. Each one of us has an inner blueprint for personal magnificence, but we have to be on the Green Platform to download it. It's there like the eagle's ability to fly was always there.

In Tolstoy's great book, "The Death of Ivan Ilyich," he introduces us to Ivan on his deathbed. Ivan was like the eagle in the hen yard. He wondered if his whole life had been a mistake. He had never achieved his true potential. He had no problem with dying. His problem was dying without having really lived.

Like the eagle, he never woke up to his own greatness. Ivan's life was a classic case again of living that famous line of Melville's in Moby Dick: "Surrounded by all the horrors of the half-lived life."

Or as winning Ryder Cup captain Jose Maria Olazabal said some time ago in the wake of his team's famous victory: "All men die but not every man lives and you made me feel alive again this week."

Howard Thurman puts it this way: "Do not ask what the world

needs. Rather ask what is it that brings you fully alive. Because you, fully alive, is what the world needs."

You fully alive on the Green Platform is what the world needs. You waking up to your greatness is what the world needs. You being the best that you can be in the service of humanity is what the world needs.

Don't miss the gorge. Or now shouldn't we change that to: "Be fully alive, here, now every step of the way on your journey through the gorge of life."

Give up liking your bad days on the Red Platform. Dare to give children the idea that some adults are actually enjoying themselves.

The single most radical revolutionary act you can commit in today's world is to dare to be a joyful person – to dare to live on the Green Platform all day every day – to dare to be the magical wonderful person you were born to be – to dare to be the best that you can be and achieve your full potential.

The greatest gift you can give to your family, your friends and your colleagues at work is your positive emotional state. Your greatest gift to them is you, fully alive on the Green Platform.

The Green Platform is nothing new. There have been literally millions of amazing people all over the world who have lived all their lives on the Green Platform without even being aware of it. Those people are the ones who have inspired us all. Always positive. Always uplifting. Always living with joy and bringing joy to others. Ordinary people living extraordinary lives. All over the place. You know who they are. You can name them right now.

Finally, on the Green Platform you will find your treasure that lies waiting. And if you are truly open to it, on the Green Platform, your treasure will also find you.

Acknowledgements

THE late John O'Donohue asked a very profound question shortly before he died: "When was the last time you had a great and powerful conversation with someone that resonated through your mind and heart and soul for weeks afterwards?"

Well, I've been lucky enough to have had several such conversations over the years with many great people I've been privileged to meet on my journey through life. I'm immensely grateful to each one of them, because the echo of their conversations resonates through this book. They were all living on the Green Platform and they have inspired me.

Growing up in Dungimmon, I was lucky enough to listen to the stories and learn the wisdom of the people in this magical part of Counties Cavan and Meath. I thank them and my own family for their unwavering support, love and friendship through all the ups and downs of life.

The next part of my life was spent with the Columban missionaries. In St Columban's College, at the foot of the hill of Tara, we had some of the best and the brightest of Ireland's students and professors. They inspired me, opened up my mind to discover new landscapes and dream impossible dreams of justice for the oppressed and food for the hungry in the far corners of the globe. I thank them.

Next came post-graduate studies in Ottawa where people like Fr Roger Lapointe and Fr Frank van der Hoff challenged us to be genuine good news for the poor, and liberation for the oppressed by not just tinkering with the symptoms of poverty, but tackling the root causes. They opened up new gospel scenarios that later on took me to the slums of the Philippines and Taiwan. I thank them profoundly.

But the man who really made a lasting impression on me and on this book is Victor Frankl, then a visiting professor to St Paul's University. His concept of the last and the greatest of the human freedoms, the "power to choose" that he discovered in the death camps of Auschwitz was and is the seed at the heart of the Green and Red Platform concepts. I am grateful to him and his family in Vienna who many years ago offered their support.

I thank the people I served in the Philippines and Taiwan. I went out to evangelise them. Instead, they evangelised me and taught me what really matters in life. Like St Francis, they insisted that we must preach the gospel but only if absolutely necessary use words. I am indebted to them and so many Columbans, Jesuits and Redemptorists who struggled with them with total solidarity in their quest for justice, food and hope.

One Australian Columban in particular I would like to thank is Fr Warren Kinne. He introduced me to my Queensland wife Annette (his sister), the mother of our three children, Genevieve, Fionn and Alexander. Their patience, support and encouragement throughout the writing of this book have been absolutely enormous.

I've been privileged to have attended many workshops and seminars with Myles O'Reilly S.J., Dick McHugh S.J., Helen Palmer (who taught us the meditation technique used in The Green Platform), the late Lou Tice RIP, Tony Robbins, Brian Tracy, Jack Canfield, Deepak Chopra, Richard Bandler, Paul McKenna, Eckhart Tolle, Robert Holden, Aidan Higgins and many more. I am grateful to them all and always learned something new from each of them about our amazing human drama.

I've always loved sport and many of the tools in this book have been tested on various football and hurling pitches here in Ireland and also on basketball courts across America.

If you want conversations that resonate and found their way into this book, then the conversations I've been privileged to have with Jack O'Connor, Paddy O'Rourke, Liam Sheedy, Anthony Daly, Richie Stakelum, Tony Griffin, Conor Counihan, Terry Hyland, Anthony Ford, Damien Sheridan, John Calipari and Paddy Carr all qualify. My sincere thanks to each one of them.

The tools in the book have been refined though my work in the corporate world with many companies across the globe. One company in particular stands out. Alltech, the global animal health and nutrition company. Since 1997 we have worked together to refine the Green Platform tools and build peak performing teams all over the world.

Over hundreds of hours of early morning runs in the US and all over the world, many of the ideas here emerged from conversations with the Alltech president, Dr Pearse Lyons, a man who has lived all his life on the Green Platform. I thank Alltech and I thank him, his wife Deirdre, his son Mark and daughter Aoife for their Green Platform insights, friendship and hospitality.

I would like to thank my brother Vincent for an initial proofreading of the manuscript and absolutely taking no prisoners when he discovered typos or grammatically incorrect bits and pieces. My thanks to Jim Martin for a final proofread and comments that took me over the line. To Nick O'Neill, a great work colleague, who has believed in this project for over a decade and to Tom Flood who always calls the odds in favour of the Green Platform.

To my neighbour, friend and great Leitrim man, Hugh McPartlan, for providing enthusiasm in abundance when my own supply was low.

Step forward too Annette van Lochem because you were the catalyst which finally brought home to me how this book could actually help people in their daily lives.

To journalist Rosemary O'Grady and Barry Cunningham in the Ballpoint Press stable I offer a sincere thanks for their attention to detail through these pages.

Also in that parish to PJ Cunningham, my editor. Without you, there simply would be no book.

Finally thanks to all of you who have shared so many touching and beautiful stories about how the Green Platform changed and transformed your lives.

Declan Coyle

Index